TEXTILE
VISIONARIES

For Carla Feldshuh

LAURENCE KING

Published in 2013
by Laurence King Publishing Ltd
361–373 City Road
London EC1V 1LR
Tel +44 20 7841 6900
Fax +44 20 7841 6910
E-mail enquiries@laurenceking.com
www.laurenceking.com

A catalogue record for this book is available from the British Library.

ISBN 978 1 78067 053 9

Designed by Charlotte Heal
Cover design by Charlie Bolton
Project editor: Gaynor Sermon
Copy editor: Lindsay Kaubi

Printed in China

TEXTILE VISIONARIES

INNOVATION AND SUSTAINABILITY IN TEXTILE DESIGN

BRADLEY QUINN

Laurence King Publishing

CONTENTS

Introduction

INTRODUCTION

MAIN PICTURE / Aurélie Mossé's Mille-feuille table features textile layers to be removed, one after the other, to change the look of the table. Each removed layer can be re-used for other decorative purposes.

FAR RIGHT, TOP TO BOTTOM / Lucy McRae's 'metabollic skin' merges body and textiles; iPad-generated textile pattern by Sheree Dornan; Kelsey Ashe's prints and motifs celebrate culture and the environment. Shown here is her Tahini Church Cheongsam print.

TEXTILES, AS WE know them today, are already becoming a thing of the past. A fresh dialogue is unfolding between the fabrics we wear and the technologies we use. Future fabrics will make us faster, lighter, brighter, greener and cleaner. They will provide us with multi-sensory skins and wearable technologies, yet be comfortable, breathable, elastic and protective. Textiles will equip the wearer with completely new physical and intellectual abilities, or enhance existing ones. Future textiles will be fully customizable and able to change colour and shape, as well as create exciting new textures. Transformable designs will enable a single textile to fulfil multiple roles. Fabrics will change shape to keep the wearer comfortable and reconfigure to meet the needs of the activities they face. Smart systems will be integrated into the fabrics we wear, effortlessly merging our personal and professional selves as they help make everyday life flow more smoothly.

Right now, fresh approaches to creating and consuming textiles are revolutionizing the use, function, life cycle and disposal of clothing and interior fabrics. Advanced fibres make fabrics more durable, while bio-materials can create resilient textures and stain-resistant surfaces. Leading designers are already advocating a holistic, cradle-to-cradle approach that considers the textile's entire life cycle, and minimizes its environmental impact. By combining sustainability and innovation, designers are finding ways to make fashion fabrics tougher and longer lasting. Smart materials will keep clothing fresh without washing, and ironing will become a thing of the past. As this new generation of textiles dawns, this book sets out to explore some of the designs that are taking the industry in new directions. Beginning with a look at textiles that integrate technological systems with everyday apparel and performance garments, section one reveals how electronic textiles can enable clothing to function like computing devices and transmit data via conductors, switches and sensors. Tiny silicon chips and sensors can be downscaled to fibre-size and interwoven with plastic-threaded chip carriers and minute circuit boards. The wearable hardware that these textiles create can sustain a range of software applications, and like most computer devices, easily adapt to changes in the computational and sensing requirements of an application.

Many of the new developments in textile designs are driven by consumer concerns about sustainability and the environment. Many of the designers featured in section two are looking at living systems to find ways of developing textiles based on processes that occur in the natural world. As a result, eco-fabrics are shrugging off their image of hemp-heavy textures and rough-and-ready surfaces, the new generation of sustainable textiles are as beautiful to the eye as they are gentle to the earth.

The textiles featured in section three are derived from surprising processes, revealing the extent to which technology and disciplines such as science can come together in fabric form. The everyday phenomenon of light and the natural occurrence of heat can be used to enable surfaces that change colourways and silhouettes that shift shape. Such innovations are bringing practitioners in a range of different fields together, changing the way that textiles are designed and used.

As a new generation of designers envisions the forms, shapes and materials of tomorrow, textiles are being transformed from passive substrates into active technological tools. Future textiles will connect individuals with wider systems as well as each other, and enrich their lives in ways we never could have imagined before. Like the skin we were born with, the hi-tech textiles we wear in future will be sensual and beautiful, fit perfectly, and feel completely natural.

TECHNOLOGY

TEXTILES AND TECHNOLOGY are made for each other. The flexible wires created for computer hardware are, in essence, conductive fibres, and the programmable components embedded into a circuit board can just as easily be embroidered onto a textile's surface. Lightweight, soft and comfortable against the skin, fabric makes a better material for portable technology than hard plastic covers or cold metal casings. Fast-paced technological advances and edgy new designs give technology a cutting-edge aesthetic, even keeping pace with fashion trends as they change from season to season.

A new generation of textile designers is emerging today, and as they find inspiration in technological systems, they align with other disciplines to find the means to create them. Some have been trained in textile design, but many of the practitioners taking the discipline forward come from other backgrounds. Among the most radical textile designs today are those engineered by scientists, designed in collaboration with technologists and programmed by computer engineers. Their input gives the discipline a broader frame of reference, and creates more scope for textiles to move in new directions. As practitioners from other disciplines find fresh applications for traditional materials and textile techniques, new ways to make, wear and live with fabric are beginning to emerge.

Cutting-edge textile research is enabling a new dialogue between body and apparel to unfold, driven by fashion's potential to function as a technological device. The fashion genres referred to variously as 'techno fashion', 'wearables' and 'techwear' are transforming textiles from passive receivers into active technological tools. Researchers are finding ways to make electronic fabrics flexible, washable and powered by a

portable energy source, which will also pave the way for new types of interior textiles to evolve. Far from making traditional craft techniques redundant, such high-tech innovations are reviving practices such as knitting, crochet and embroidery. As they do so, they explore the extent to which fibre structures and surface embellishments can provide new ways of transmitting data.

The fabrics of tomorrow will not be textiles as we know them today. While technological expert Leah Buechley creates future roles for time-honoured textile design techniques, practitioners such as Despina Papadopoulos, Valérie Lamontagne and Sabine Seymour are creating DIY kits that can transform almost any fabric into an electronic textile. Designers such as Nancy Tilbury and Lucy McRae are preparing for a day when clothing will emerge from rapid-assembly gases, and active nanoparticles will be suspended in a liquid solution. If rapid-assembly particles can form textiles around the body, they may make fashion fabrics redundant. They could also be engineered to create a particle cloud that will form a textile surface when it comes into contact with other types of objects, such as furniture or architectural components.

This section features the work of 12 practitioners whose innovative approach is pioneering new directions for fashion textiles. In their hands, fashion fabrics will soon shrug off their low-tech trademarks and embrace the wireless future, becoming one of the most expressive examples of technology today.

RIGHT / Layne's spectacular Tornado Dress features a Mimaki print of a tornado whirling across the garment's surface. Photocells that detect light trigger the LEDs to flash in order to mimic lighting.

BARBARA LAYNE

Alvin Toffler, the prophet of the digital revolution, wrote in his seminal book *Future Shock* in 1970 that the shock of the new resulted from 'too much change in too short a period of time'. Since then, the meteoric rise of digitally enhanced textiles has gained momentum at a speed that even Toffler would find hard to fathom. Although the new generation of electronic fabrics has yet to establish a market, the timing for a digital textile revolution couldn't be more perfect.

When North American textile designer Barbara Layne considered the future of fabric, she viewed it in terms of systems and electronics more than fibres and fluff. As a result, Layne began creating receptive surfaces that can transmit data and respond to external stimuli. Experiments with LEDs led to garments that change patterns and broadcast texts through the structure of cloth. Layne interweaves circuits with natural fibres to create soft surfaces that function like microcomputers. Equipped with wireless transmission systems, Layne's designs have also been developed to support real-time communication between wearers.

Layne's impact on the industry has been considerable, and as a professor at Concordia University in Montreal and a founding member of Hexagram, a research institute for new media and technology, her reach spans academia as well as the arts. At Hexagram, Layne founded Studio subTela, one of

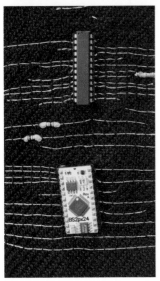

ABOVE / This close-up reveals how intricately the garment's circuitry is embedded within the textile.

TOP / Layne and her team created two light-emitting jackets that rely on physical contact with each other in order to trigger encoded signals to scroll through LED arrays embedded on the surface.

ABOVE / Barbara Layne and Yacov Sharir collaborated to create this LED jacket for the Twining Initiative, a dance project examining how new wearable interactive systems can affect onstage interaction and offer new communication possibilities with the audience.

five studio-laboratories working with innovative textiles. The name was not chosen arbitrarily: 'subTela comes from Latin, meaning "under the cloth",' Layne explains, 'which refers to small threads that support larger decorative elements in the fabric. The name seems quite fitting as it describes the weave structure we developed that holds the electronic components on the surface in a way that prevents short circuits.'

Layne and her team designed two light-emitting jackets that debuted at the Integration exhibition held at the Simon Dougherty Gallery in Sydney, in Spring 2007. Interactive and chic, Layne named the designs 'Jacket Antics' and describes the pair as 'mated' because they rely on physical contact with each other in order to trigger a range of dynamically encoded signals that scroll through their LED arrays. Layne and her team also created the tempestuous 'Tornado Dress', which features a Mimaki print of a tornado whirling across the surface. The dress is equipped with photocells that detect light, and the lining has been embroidered with conductive threads, electronic components and super-bright white LEDs. 'The quantity of light the photocells detect triggers flashing patterns in the LED display,' Layne explains, 'which mimic lightning.'

Other types of interactive technology are being adapted for a system of garments and interior panels equipped with a Bluetooth technology, called 'Currente Calamo', that enables them to communicate with each other wirelessly. Layne and her team are developing a touchpad system to trigger changing designs and texts in a flexible LED array. 'This is a real-time system that explores both intimate and architectural scale hand-woven cloth with embedded soft touchpads that relay the output to LED devices,' Layne explains. 'The touchpad system will quite literally respond at the touch of a finger, creating a system of interchangeable garments and interior fabrics responsive to human interaction.'

Despite her innovative approach, Layne does not necessarily see her work as groundbreaking. 'Electronic textiles will function in society as part of the ongoing evolution of textiles throughout history,' she says. 'Textile innovation has existed for millennia, with each society adding new layers of text or design. Electronic fabrics may seem to have new functions but they are carriers of cultural information, just as textiles always have been throughout time.'

LEFT / Layne devised ways of weaving miniature LEDs into fabric to make it illuminate. Weaving them into the fabric makes them an integral part of the textile. Communication technology makes it possible for the wearer to receive messages.

OPPOSITE, TOP / Because the LEDs that form the display on the Currente Calamo are spaced apart, texts are easier to read when they are sent one word at a time.

OPPOSITE, BELOW / This detail from the Currente Calamo jacket shows how letters scroll across the display to form words.

ABOVE / Layne's Currente Calamo collection includes a cap-sleeved dress and a jacket with integrated digital displays. The garments shown here were exhibited at the Kaunas Textile Biennale in 2011.

RIGHT / As well as displaying written messages, the Currente Calamo dress can also receive symbols and project them across the surface. Here, the dress displays a pair of crossed hockey sticks.

ABOVE / The Jacket Antic garments can transmit texts and symbols through the LED displays on their backs. When the wearers hold hands the texts scroll from one jacket to the other.

Layne's vision of future fabric is taking shape through technological systems and electronic components, making fibres and fluff a thing of the past.

LEFT, ALL IMAGES / As this couple wearing Jacket Antics interact, the physical contact between them links them so that their respective digital displays function as one. When they break apart, the displays automatically begin to transmit individual messages.

BELOW / This LED jacket was created for the Twining Initiative, a collaborative project between Layne and choreographer-dancer Yacov Sharir.

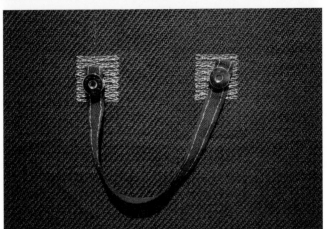

TOP LEFT / A short version of Jacket Antics, shown on the previous pages, featuring the trademark LED display.

TOP RIGHT & ABOVE / Woven into black fabric, the Blue Code display is programmed to project a variety of patterns. The viewer can interact with the fabric to trigger new patterns to be displayed. Blue Code is made with a hand-woven display consisting of nearly 400 LEDs and a panel containing eight pairs of conductive squares. When the two are linked, the pattern transmitted across the display changes.

ABOVE / This close-up of one of Blue Code's connectors shows how conductive thread is used to link them.

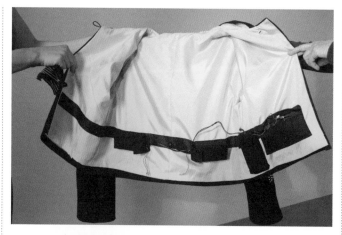

LEFT, ALL IMAGES / This jacket was made for the Wearable Absence project in collaboration with Janis Jefferies. It is embedded with bio-sensors that detect different emotional states that the wearer experiences. Depending on the emotion the bio-sensors identify, the garment triggers audio loops, scrolling video projections, still images and texts to appear on the surface.

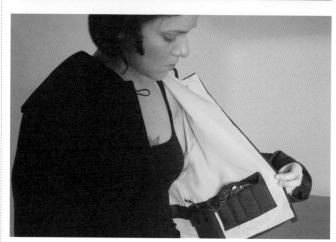

ABOVE / The jacket is connected to an online database via a handheld device that activates rich media files and streams them into the garment wirelessly.

ABOVE LEFT & RIGHT /
Layne used a Jacquard structure to create the Lucere wall hanging, which has a duotone black-and-white landscape. The wall hanging depicts an image of a tornado and lightening bolts, based on a photograph taken by Mike Hollingshead.

RIGHT & FAR RIGHT /
A microcontroller and sonic sensor are woven into the fabric to make it responsive to external stimuli. The presence of individuals near it can trigger the LEDs to glow, mimicking the 'heat lightening' associated with tornados.

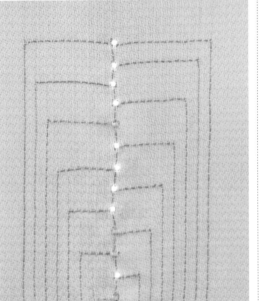

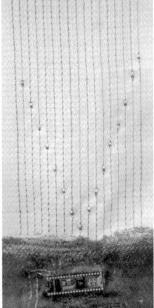

LEFT / Lightening bolts and a funnel cloud are printed on the surface of the Tornado Dress. Photocells attached to the outside of the dress trigger the LEDs to flash when they detect low light levels. The effect is that of mini lightening bolts flickering around the tornado shown on the dress's surface.

RIGHT / The Twirkle T-shirt is a simple cotton garment that sparkles and glows. Coloured LEDs are integrated into the garment alongside embroidered crystals. Motion sensors embedded in the fabric sense the wearer's movements and make the LEDs sparkle in response to them.

CUTECIRCUIT

In the ten short years that they have been active, CuteCircuit's contributions to the fashion industry have been considerable. Founding directors Francesca Rosella, an Italian fashion designer who worked previously at Valentino and Esprit, and Ryan Genz, an American design engineer, make technological garments that are beautiful to look at and comfortable to wear. Many of their designs are considered to be groundbreaking in their combinations of textiles and technology, not least because they have been worn by Hollywood celebrities and international pop stars such as U2 and Katy Perry. Rosella and Genz are based in a studio in London, but travel worldwide creating performance costumes, making museum pieces and designing private commissions, alongside the CuteCircuit ready-to-wear collection.

Each of CuteCircuit's designs begins at the fibre level. As Rosella and Genz consider the operable capacities of conductive fibres and the potential to integrate microelectronic systems into fashion fabrics, they merge telecommunication technology with textile design. By combining textiles with miniature LEDs, they create fashion fabrics capable of changing colour and pattern. Made into garments, and combined with integrated sensors that detect movement or body heat, the clothing that results responds to the activity of the wearer. Motion-activated garments such as the 'Kinetic Dress' respond to

ABOVE / The body-hugging Armour Dress is digitally printed with an armour pattern onto which crystals have been hand-embroidered.

specific movements that cue certain colours to emerge on the garment's surface. Considering the large number of independent microelectronic systems and integrated sensors it takes to create such effects, it's surprising that none of them are visible in the fabric itself. Whereas other examples of wearable technology bond sensors, connectors and circuit boards to fabric, resulting in hard plastic pieces, trailing wires and pockets full of batteries, CuteCircuit's creations have the look and feel of ordinary garments.

CuteCircuit were one of the first fashion labs to endow garments with characteristics that can make wearing them an emotionally rich experience. The 'Hug Shirt', a wearable

haptic interface conceived as a Bluetooth accessory for mobile phones, recreates the experience of being hugged by a loved one. 'We made the garments by integrating Bluetooth technology into the shirts,' Rosella explains, 'which enabled it to receive data from mobile phones as simply as receiving a text message. The shirts are embedded with sensors that can receive and transmit information to any smart phone. The wearers can send a simulated caress to each other by touching pressure-sensitive areas on their own shirt, using it as a wearable mouse pad to activate the pressure-sensitive areas on the recipient's shirt. The sensors monitor the pressure of the hug, the sender's heart rate, their skin temperature and the duration of the hug, and relay it to the other wearer's shirt via the mobile phone network.' Even those without a Hug Shirt can send virtual hugs to their wearers. By using a software application known as 'HugMe', a virtual hug can be created and transmitted wirelessly (via Bluetooth) and then sent as a message anywhere across the world to a recipient shirt, effectively transmitting a touch message from person to person.

To create the 'Hug' system, CuteCircuit tried out a variety of fabrics and materials, including sponges and balloons. 'We mapped out the positioning of arms and hands as people hugged each other, and recorded the positions on the textile,' Rosella says. 'Areas such as the upper arms, upper back, neck, shoulders and around the waist were fitted with detachable pads containing the hugging output actuators, which compress the fabric to create the sensation of a hug.'

CuteCircuit's groundbreaking 'Galaxy Dress' was commissioned by the Museum of Science and Industry in Chicago for their permanent collection. The dress was embroidered with 24,000 full-colour LEDs and 4,000 Swarovski crystals, making it the largest wearable digital display in the world. The dress was crafted from four layers of silk chiffon, onto which CuteCircuit embroidered the smallest LEDs available, using conductive threads to interconnect them with extra-thin, flexible circuits. 'Although the surface of the dress contained an extensive layer of technological parts, the embroidery techniques we used enabled the fabric to drape

smoothly across the body and move with lightness and fluidity,' says Rosella. 'Because the LEDs' energy consumption is low, the dress is powered by normal iPod batteries without any risk of overheating.'

Singer-songwriter Katy Perry famously commissioned a couture gown from CuteCircuit, which received much acclaim when she wore it to the annual Met Gala held at the Metropolitan Museum of Art in New York. Like the Galaxy Dress, Perry's gown was made from flowing silk chiffon and embroidered with LEDs to create a rainbow of colours shimmering all over the surface of the dress. Fashion magazines included Perry in their 'best dressed' lists, saying that her dress lit up the evening, and projected a light into fashion's future.

Future generations may look back at our era and regard CuteCircuit as one of the most significant fashion labs of our time. Rosella and Genz's ability to programme fibres, integrate communication technology and incorporate electronic pieces into garments has shown the fashion world that wearable technology can be as beautiful as it is innovative. As CuteCircuit continue to pioneer new directions for wearable technology, their textile design innovations promise to reveal new potentials in the future that may seem impossible today.

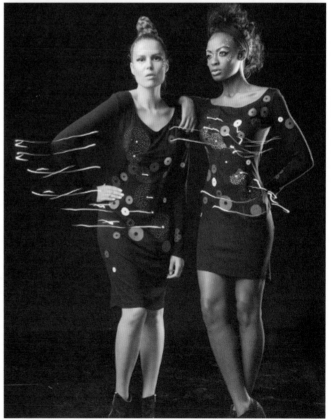

OPPOSITE PAGE, TOP / The pattern made for the Armour Dress was created to enhance the wearer's contours and curves.

OPPOSITE PAGE, BOTTOM / The Twirkle technology, shown on the T-shirt on the previous page, can be adapted for a wide range of garments for men and women. By day, the crystals sparkle in the sunlight, and at night a full-colour array of tiny LEDs twinkle and glow in response to the wearer's movements.

LEFT / The K-Dress is groundbreaking in its combinations of textiles and technology, not least because it is beautiful to look at and comfortable to wear. The dress shown here has been programmed to illuminate only the yellow-coloured LEDs.

LEFT & ABOVE / This dress was commissioned by pop star Safura to wear while performing at the Eurovision Song Contest. The dress was made from hand-pleated silk chiffon and embedded with over 5400 LEDs, programmed to illuminate in response to a video stream transmitted in real time to technology embedded in the dress.

CuteCircuit's designs contain sensors, connectors, soft circuit boards, conductive fibres and power sources, yet have the look, feel and drape of ordinary garments.

LEFT & BELOW / Both versions of the Twirkle T-shirt shown here are powered by a rechargeable battery. The battery charges via a computer USB port. A two-hour charge is usually enough to enable the shirt to sparkle for several days.

RIGHT & ABOVE / Safura's dress was programmed to follow her physical movements on stage. Subtle movements were interpreted as softly sparkling lights, which would pulsate vividly when Safura's performance became more animated. When her performance was at its most dramatic, the entire surface of the dress became brightly illuminated and vibrant.

DAVA NEWMAN

When Dava Newman sat down to design the BioSuit™, she had a whole world to invent. As a professor of Aeronautics and Astronautics and Engineering Systems at the Massachusetts Institute of Technology, Newman was well versed in bioengineering, biomechanics, human interface technologies and aerospace materials before she even accepted the assignment. Funded by the NASA Institute of Advanced Concepts to develop a new, more efficient spacesuit for future space exploration, Newman took a 'second-skin approach' to the project. Whereas previous generations of the spacesuit were made with bulky layers that cocooned the wearer in a protective gas-filled sheath, Newman's prototype spacesuit BioSuit™ is made from elastic materials that compress the human form and mould to its shape, moving with the body as the wearer walks in space or explores a planet's surface.

Newman's BioSuit™ heralds a radical departure from existing spacesuits. 'Although humans have been travelling in space for more than 40 years, the suits they wear have changed very little,' Newman says. 'Bulky, gas-pressurized suits provide astronauts with a protective life-support bubble, but their significant mass and the pressure itself severely limit mobility.' The current prototype version of the BioSuit™ is not yet ready for space travel, but demonstrates what Newman is trying to achieve. 'The BioSuit™, with its life-support systems and wearable robotic capabilities, will be needed when NASA launches an expedition to Mars, when astronauts will explore extra-terrestrial terrain,' Newman says. 'Current spacesuits cannot handle the challenges such an exploratory mission presents. When worn while making a space walk in a microgravity environment, such a massive suit is manageable. But for exploration on a planet's surface, astronauts need a suit they can walk, run and bend in.'

At a time when compression fabrics are becoming more widespread in sportswear, fashion and textile design, the BioSuit's™ pressurized environment is likely to influence terrestrial styles as much as it will space wear. 'The suit is made from a combination of ordinary materials, such as spandex and nylon, and smart materials such as shape memory alloys (Nitinol or nickel titanium),' Newman says. 'In addition to the polymer elastic materials that we are using, our smart zippers provide additional compression. Instead of using gas pressurization, which exerts force on the astronaut's body to protect it from the vacuum of space, the suit relies on mechanical counter-pressure, which involves wrapping tight layers of material around the body.' For a future flight spacesuit, the materials would need to include fabric strong enough to withstand the impact of micrometeorites and textiles that protect the wearer from high levels of radiation. The synergy between the different types of textiles used is enhanced by compression, heightening performance while remaining flexible enough to facilitate normal movements.

One of the most challenging aspects of the BioSuit™ design

RIGHT / Dava Newman, shown here in a prototype of the spacesuit she designed, created it by combining principles of bioengineering, biomechanics and human interface technologies with fabric design and tailoring techniques.

BELOW / Newman's design heralds a radical departure from the bulk that characterizes existing spacesuits. Newman took a 'second skin' approach to the project, using compression to mould the fabric to the astronaut's body.

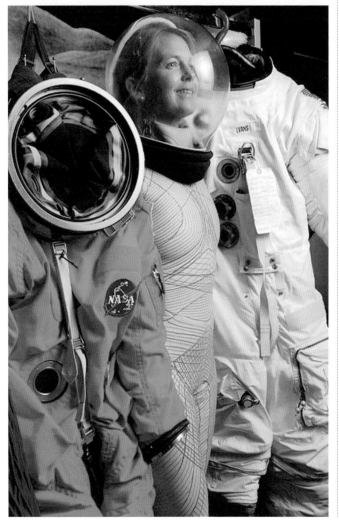

is making its arms and legs taut enough to facilitate compression while still flexible enough to easily allow movement at the knees, elbows and shoulders. Newman investigated 3D models of how human skin stretches as the body bends, climbs, walks and runs, then explored techniques such as wrapping and bias-cutting that would enable the materials to mimic the movement of the skin. The areas of skin that stretch the least when the body moves (technically known as non-extension) are reinforced by strong filaments that provide structural support to static areas, while areas that require maximal mobility have flexible supports.

Newman's research is also beneficial for Earth-bound applications, such as athletic training and physiotherapy treatments that help patients walk. 'The BioSuit™ is intended to help astronauts stay fit during the six-month journey to Mars,' Newman says. 'It could offer varying resistance levels, which the astronauts can exercise against during the long journey to Mars during IVA, or intra-vehicular activities.'

Newman says her next frontier was inspired by aerospace technology but will take place in the healthcare sector. 'The assistive devices within the BioSuit's™ legs will have the potential to assist people on Earth who need help walking,' Newman says. 'I'd like to adapt them to make a suit for children with cerebral palsy to enhance movement and help them walk.'

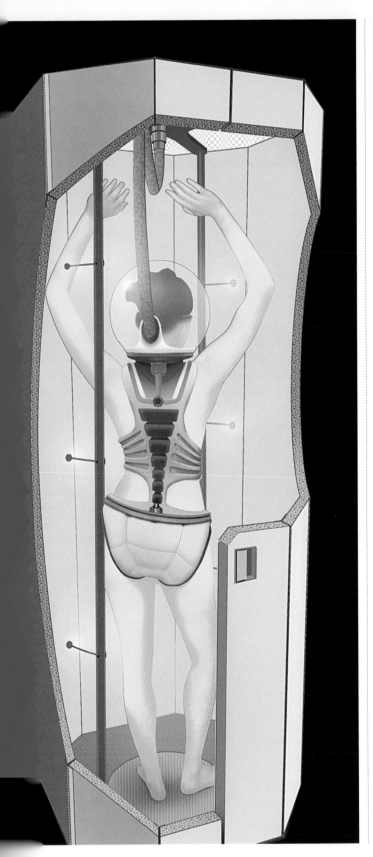

ABOVE / The BioSuit™ comprises layers of nylon, spandex and urethane that have been embedded with electronic components. The helmet is made from smart materials that regulate temperature and contain technology that facilitates communication and spatial orientation.

LEFT / The innermost layer of the BioSuit™ does not necessarily need to be put on like conventional clothing. Fibres could be suspended in an aerosol solution and sprayed on, as this rendering shows.

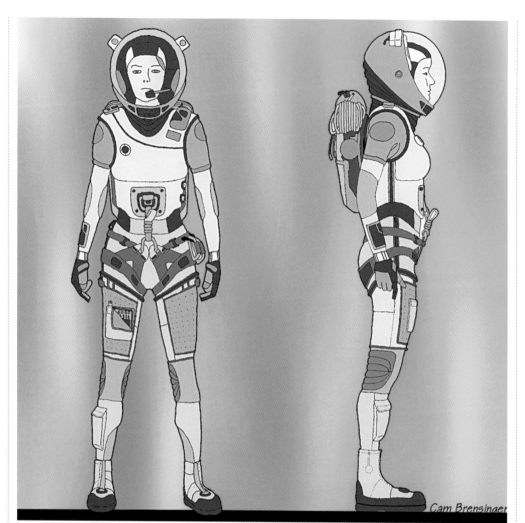

LEFT / The BioSuit™ relies on mechanical counter-pressure to make the life-support systems work. The spacesuit's tight-fitting inner layers apply pressure to the entire body. Pressure is also maintained by the helmet.

Cam Brensinger

RIGHT / Newman studied the skin's inherent elasticity to determine which areas stretch the most when the body moves. This rendering uses arrows to indicate which areas of the spacesuit provide structural support that enables the suit to contract, and which areas have flexible supports.

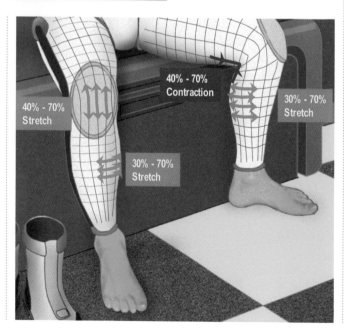

40% - 70% Stretch

40% - 70% Contraction

30% - 70% Stretch

30% - 70% Stretch

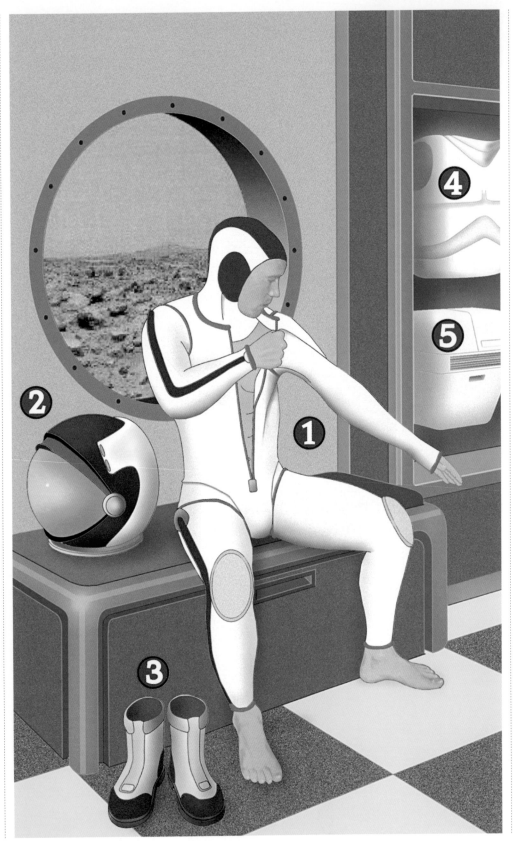

LEFT & BELOW / Newman puts on a prototype of the spacesuit to test it herself. The suit's flexible materials enable her to walk normally and stand comfortably in most conditions. Materials that promote extension enable her to bend her knees normally, while the suit's mechanical counter-pressure actually assists her as she rises to her feet again.

RIGHT & BELOW / The BioSuit™ was designed with movement in mind, which is why Newman made it from lightweight, elastic textiles and flexible materials. The renderings shown here depict astronauts establishing a space colony on the surface of Mars, wearing a suit that protects them from the planet's harsh atmosphere while enabling them to flex, bend and climb.

Newman works at the point where engineering, textile design, biochemistry and material science meet, revealing new capabilities for textiles worn in outer space and on Earth.

ABOVE / Newman works at the intersection of engineering, textile design, medicine and material science. Her research reveals new roles and capabilities for textiles worn in outer space and on Earth.

DESPINA PAPADOPOULOS

Founder of Studio 5050 and a leader in the field of wearable electronics, Despina Papadopoulos teaches on New York University's Interactive Telecommunications Program and has written extensively about the integration of technology and fashion fabrics. Together with her Studio 5050 colleagues, Papadopoulos has designed surface-mounted computer components that attach to textiles, and flexible circuits that could be woven into fabric. Papadopoulos has also experimented with weaving conductive threads in a Jacquard loom, producing fabrics for fashion and interior applications that are capable of transmitting electronic signals.

The driving force behind Papadopoulos' designs appears to be her ability to find new ways of connecting people to their surroundings and to each other. Whereas garments are often seen as individual shells that shield the wearer from their surroundings, Papadopoulos' wearable textiles bring them closer together. Her 'Masai Dress' is made from a textile embellished with conductive threads, and features a collar formed by strings of handmade silver beads. As the beads brush against the conductive fibres, they trigger a variety of pre-programmed sounds. 'With each step, speakers in the dress emit sounds created by the synergy between the conductive fibres and the silver beads,' Papadopoulos explains. 'The sounds are generated by the wearer's movements, which when walking, indicate when they are climbing steps, changing their gait or stumbling across

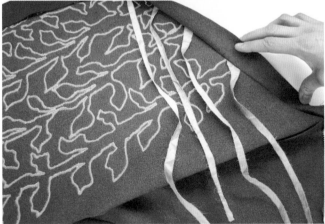

TOP / Papadopoulos and Zach Eveland created Fabrickit, a starter toolbox that designers can use to make their textiles interactive. The LED components shown here have been linked to sensors that trigger them to illuminate, and they have been connected to a wearable power source.

ABOVE / Papadopoulos uses conductive ribbons in wearable applications to make garments interactive.

uneven terrain.' 'Masai' reveals that separate textile layers can interact to create an auditory rendering of the wearer's movements in the space around them.

As Papadopoulos works on engineering wearable textiles that relate individuals to the spaces around them, she also designs garments that reflect and promote social interactions. Together with her colleagues at Studio 5050, Papadopoulos created the 'Hug Jackets', a pair of lightweight outer garments designed to emit and track a specific signal broadcast on a particular frequency. The jackets were kitted out with a basic infrared receiver and transmitter, LED panels, a PIC micro-controller chip and a speaker output. The components were surface-mounted and

interconnected via conductive fibres woven into the fabric, but, as the prototypes continue to evolve, the technology will become seamlessly integrated into the fabric.

The jackets were programmed to identify and track the same wave frequency they are emitting. The speaker output enables the jacket to broadcast the specific code assigned to it, and when it comes within a three-metre range of an identical code being broadcast, it locks onto it. 'The jackets respond by emitting bleeping noises, simultaneously triggering a pattern of LEDs to begin blinking on the surface,' Papadopoulos explains. 'The jackets are only programmed to identify and respond to the other counterpart in its pair. The jackets may appear to visibly recognize their counterparts, but actually, the infrared operates on an invisible spectrum, similar to a remote control device. Because the polling distance is short-range, the jackets have to come within "sight" of each other to be detected.' Once the jackets have identified each other's wave frequency, the wearers will be within visual range of each other, and will recognize the other half of the pair.

Papadopoulos claims that integrating technology into textiles is easier than most designers realize, and has even created a 'toolbox' that they can use to get started. In collaboration with Blacklabel, the Brooklyn-based electronic design consultancy, and her colleagues at Studio 5050, Papadopoulos launched 'fabrickit', a collection of technical components that enable designers to make wearable electronics. The fabrickit system has been designed with flexibility and modularity in mind, which makes the construction of technological fabrics easy enough for beginners. Fabrickit provides a set of electronic components that can be incorporated into interior textiles, fashion fabrics and readymade garments. The collection consists of a flexible, three-wire conductive fabric ribbon, a removable, rechargeable coin cell battery, an LED module with built-in resistor, snap connectors, switches and breakout boards.

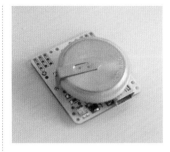

ABOVE / Part of the fabrickit set, the coin cell module shown here is a tiny rechargeable power source that can be integrated into fabric. The module is a 5-volt energy source that can power LED components.

RIGHT / This is a photograph of the Hug Jacket. A pre-cursor to fabrickit, it uses a similar conductive ribbon.

OPPOSITE, TOP / This electronic component contains an LED and can be sewn into a garment like any other kind of embellishment. Linked to sensors, accelerometers or microcontrollers, they can be programmed to blink, pulsate or remain illuminated.

OPPOSITE, BELOW / Despina Papadopoulos and Zach Eveland created fabrickit, a starter toolbox that designers can use to make their textiles interactive. Fabrickit includes a removable, rechargeable coin cell battery module, LED modules with built-in resistors and a snap connector module.

Papadopoulos' work connects people to their surroundings and to each other. Rather than design individual garments, she develops wearable networks that bring people closer.

LEFT / Fabrickit's snap connector module, shown here, makes connections between different electronic components quick and easy to create.

BELOW LEFT / Fabrickit contains flexible ribbon, shown here in the Hug Jacket, which is made from tinsel wire and polyester that can be used to connect the electronic components. The ribbon can also be used as seam tape.

BELOW RIGHT / Thin pieces of conductive fabric is used to sense when the two jackets make contact with each other.

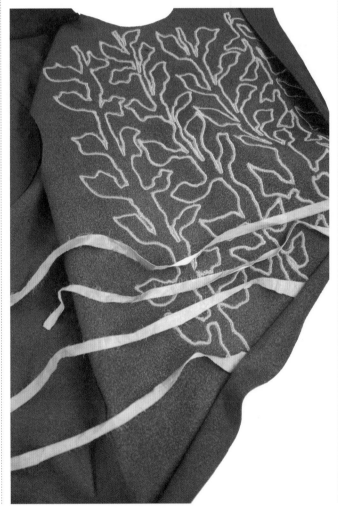

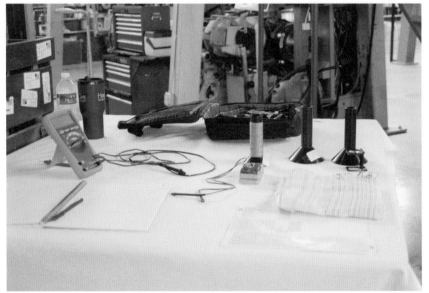

ABOVE / Papadopoulos carried out research at Oriole Mill in North Carolina, where she developed methods of incorporating conductive threads in a Jacquard loom. As a result, Papadopoulos produced woven fabrics capable of transmitting electronic signals.

LEFT / At Oriole Mill, Papadopoulos equipped her workbench with conductive thread, electrical testing equipment, a sample of woven fabric and a voltmeter.

RIGHT / Berzowska's Modular
Pleated Lights Dress was developed
in collaboration with the Advanced
Photonic Structures Group in
Montréal. The dress harnesses the
energy generated by the human body
and uses it to power the changes
on the surface.

JOANNA BERZOWSKA

Joanna Berzowska is the founder of XS Labs, a textile research studio established in 2002 to develop electronic textiles and responsive garments. Based in Montréal, Berzowska is also an associate professor of Design and Computation Arts at Concordia University and a member of the Hexagram Research Institute. Berzowska's approach to design is transgressive, often flirting subtly with elements of the absurd, the perverse and the unknown. 'I construct narratives that involve dark humour and romanticism as a way to drive design innovation,' she says. 'These integrative approaches allow us to construct composite textiles with complex functionality and sophisticated behaviours.'

XS stands for X-tra Soft, and a core component of Berzowska's research is the development of soft electronic circuits, composite fibres and tactile substrates that can be worn comfortably against the skin. Berzowska's interest in the field was not inspired by weaving, fashion, fabric design or even fibre arts, but from a resolve to address the lack of softness and tactility in human–computer interactions. 'While a student at the MIT Media Lab in the mid-1990s, I was drawn to electronic textiles for their ability to conform to the human body and their potential for bringing softness to computer interfaces,' she says. Today Berzowska's work highlights how designers working in the IT and telecommunication industries continue to limit their output to traditional definitions

LEFT / The dress is constructed with fibre optic strands that illuminate when worn. Connected to an LED light source, the fibre optics can emit a range of colours.

BELOW / The dress is equipped with a control panel that enables the wearer to regulate power levels, initiate surges of light and send subtle pulses of colour through the fabric.

ABOVE / Berzowska says that weaving thin strands of fibre optics together with conventional yarn is somewhat challenging, but the unique textures that result make it well worth the effort.

of computers and their intended uses, without considering ergonomic needs and the wide range of materials available. 'My projects consider the soft, playful and tactile aspects of wearable materials, which easily adapt to the contours of the human body and the complexities of human needs and desires,' she says.

Many of Berzowska's electronic innovations are informed by the technical history and cultural traditions associated with textile practices. She explains: 'Techniques such as weaving, stitching, embroidery, knitting, beading or quilting have the potential to embellish a textile surface as well as create a soft, reactive structure that has electro-mechanical properties.' One of Berzowska's key research interests is the area she calls 'human-generated power', which has inspired garments such as her 'Constellation Dresses', designed to bring people together physically and electronically. Covered with 12 pairs of magnetic snaps connected by a single line of embroidered conductive thread, the dresses are studded with LEDs that resemble clusters of interconnected stars. One set of metallic snaps acts as a switch for the LED circuit, which, when connected to the corresponding snaps on another dress, closes the circuit to light up the LEDs. The snaps function as a mechanical and electrical connection between the wearers, which are positioned on the dress in places that encourage wearers to create playful arrangements in order to connect their circuits.

'Rather than being complete and functional electronic pieces in themselves, the dresses work as meshes on a circuit network and depend on the physical contact of the magnetic snaps to function,' she explains. 'The dresses compel people to draw power from each other, hinting at a parasitic model for powering our mobile technologies and suggesting metaphors for building electronic or social networks.'

The energy needed to provide power for technological textiles can be drawn from the body itself. Berzowska's 'Captain Electric and Battery Boy' initiative was set up to create electronic garments that harness energy passively from the body and make it available to the user. Garments equipped with accelerators can produce an electric charge whenever the body moves, then transmit it to energy coils where, like a battery, it can be stored until needed.

Berzowska is collaborating with a research group set up by Maksim Skorobogatiy at the Polytechnique Montréal to develop new types of technical fibres for biomedical and sensing applications and find applications for them. 'We have been using the Jacquard loom to develop new weave structures using photonic bandgap Bragg fibres for applications in interactive garments, interior design, sensing fabrics, signage and works of art,' she says. 'These fibres can be compared to optical fibres, but they have very different visual characteristics. Under ambient illumination, the fibres appear coloured due to their microstructure even though no dyes or colourants are used

OPPOSITE PAGE / Berzowska's Skorpions designs are a collection of electronic garments that slowly morph into new shapes. They are intended to adapt to the wearer's behaviour by creating protective shells or inviting playful interactions.

TOP & BOTTOM LEFT / The Skorpions movements are triggered by the kinetic energy created by the body, causing the garments to shift and change in ways that the wearer doesn't anticipate.

BOTTOM RIGHT / The Captain Electric series of garments can be powered by harnessing the body's energy or propelled by the energy released when the wearer manipulates the tubes and pulleys embedded into them.

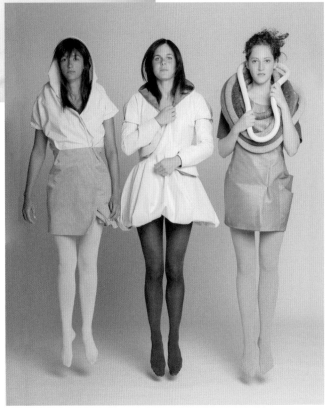

in their fabrication. When a high-brightness LED is used to transmit white light through the fibre, it illuminates in colour. The coloured light is visible without the need for bending or abrasion, as is necessary for fibre optics.'

As Berzowska and her team at XS Labs explore the use of conductive fibres, photoelectrics, LEDs and shape-memory materials their output is creating a new generation of electronic textiles. The garments they create redefine human–computer interactions, highlighting the importance of user experience and the roles that tactility and ergonomics can play. 'Our design philosophy focuses on the use of transitive materials and technologies,' Berzowska says. 'We're participating in a scientific revolution that has begun to redefine fundamental design methods.'

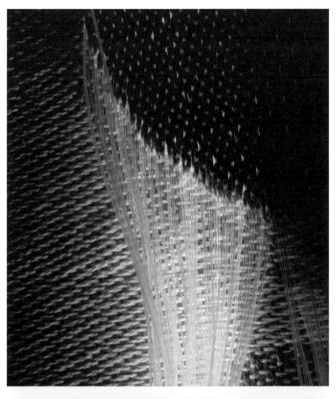

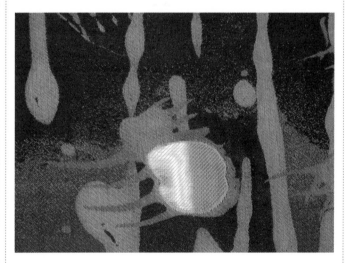

OPPOSITE PAGE / Berzowska's Captain Electric research project aims to develop electronic garments that harness body energy to power electronic components integrated into the fabric. The garments shown here are prototypes developed for the project.

THIS PAGE / The composite fibres shown here are able to harness energy directly from the human body, store that energy, and then use it to change their appearance. Created for the Karma Chameleon collection, the fibres are able to illuminate, and change colour and luminosity in response to the wearer's movements.

Berzowska's approach to design is transgressive, often flirting subtly with elements of the absurd, the perverse, and the unknown.

RIGHT & BELOW / The Skorpions garments are constructed using traditional textile techniques such as folding, pleating and draping, yet are crafted from groundbreaking materials. Electronic fabrics, the shape-memory alloy Nitinol, mechanical actuators and soft electronic circuitry enable the fabric to move, unfold and redrape itself around the wearer's body.

ABOVE & RIGHT / The Sparkl panels are created on a computer-operated Jacquard loom where they are woven with linen, cotton and photonic bandgap (PBG) fibres. The colours reflected by the photonic bandgap fibres depend on the type of light they are programmed to transmit. As a result, different layers of imagery and colour are revealed.

RIGHT / The Living Wall project, led by Leah Buechley, developed electronically-enhanced wallpaper. The wallpaper uses magnetic pigments and conductive paints to create circuitry embedded in the surface motif. The wallpaper is interlinked with other household objects, such as table lamps and music systems. Touching different parts of the surface triggers them to switch on and off.

LEAH BUECHLEY

RIGHT / The motifs are sketched out by hand before being coloured with conductive paints.

FAR RIGHT / Also developed for the Living Wall project, this wallpaper can be programmed to control lighting and sound. As it provides a decorative function, it provides an unobtrusive way to integrate electronics within the home.

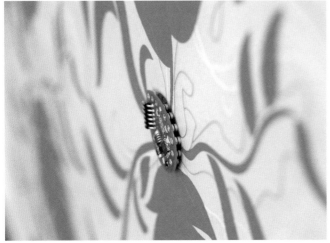

At the cutting edge of high-tech design and textile technology, much of Leah Buechley's work is characterized by the use of traditional crafts and unassuming materials. As an assistant professor at the MIT Media Lab and director of the MIT's High-Low Tech Research Group, Buechley is surrounded by some of the most pioneering technologies being developed today. Although many others working in the field take user interfaces as their starting point, Buechley's work is less about designing new consumer devices, and more about developing new tools and new ways of working.

The High-Low Tech Research Group was established to explore the extent to which advanced technology and traditional craftsmanship can come together. Textiles, with their tradition of hand-craftsmanship and high-tech applications, provide the perfect medium for Buechley and her colleagues to experiment with. Buechley approaches textiles from cultural, material and practical perspectives, and transforms them into technological substrates that people of all ages and cultural backgrounds can relate to and create for themselves. 'My primary goal is to reach out to diverse groups and show them how to design and build their own technologies,' Buechley explains. 'I believe that future technology will be largely created by people who will design and build their own devices. At the High-Low Tech Research Group, we endeavour to inspire, shape and support these communities.'

Buechley's approach is changing the way that technology is investigated and understood. Whereas the fabrication of computational devices usually requires a set of technological skills and an assortment of factory-produced hardware components, Buechley's system makes it possible to craft simple machines from fibre-based parts. 'We are exploring ways to build electronic devices using a variety of crafting and needlework techniques, using materials such as conductive threads, yarns, fabrics and paints,' Buechley explains. 'These materials are used to sew, knit, crochet and embroider a range of soft, textile-based devices.'

Buechley designed a toolkit that contains soft electronic components that can be integrated into fabric to create tailor-made interactive devices. Named 'LilyPad Arduino', the kit includes a small, sew-able computer (an Arduino microcontroller) and an assortment of sew-able sensors (light and temperature sensors) and actuators (motors, lights and speakers). Buechley incorporated the LilyPad Arduino into her 'Turn Signal' cycling jacket, which features arrow-shaped turn indicators integrated within the fabric on the back. By squeezing the switches sewn into the cuffs, the arrows can be triggered to point either right or left to show the direction the cyclist will turn in. 'Lights in the cuffs illuminate as soon as the arrows are activated,' Buechley explains, 'which gives the wearers immediate feedback. That way, they will know that the arrow has been turned on and then off again.' The system can also be used to enhance the cyclist's visibility at night. 'Pressing both of the cuff switches at the same time triggers both arrows to flash simultaneously, making it much easier for the cyclist to be seen by cars.'

Thousands of people around the world are using the LilyPad Arduino kit to build their own interactive electronic textiles, including variations on the Turn Signal jacket. It has sparked a new and growing do-it-yourself movement in textiles and technology that Buechley and her students continue to research and support.

Wearable LED displays also feature in Buechley's beaded LED bracelets, which are woven out of LEDs, glass beads and conductive thread and function as programmable display matrices. The bracelets are woven on a traditional bead loom before being programmed with patterns of animated lights. In one design, movement activates mathematical patterns called cellular automata. Buechley explains that, 'the shaking of the wrist is detected by an accelerometer, triggering the cellular automaton pattern. The accelerometer can also detect the incline of the arm. When the bracelet is held upright for a few seconds, the pattern freezes. Tilting the arm downward again initiates a new pattern sequence.'

The projects and prototypes Buechley develops are creating new relationships between craft forms and technological systems. As she develops new interactions between traditional textile techniques and high-tech designs, Buechley is also pioneering new horizons for both.

ABOVE / Buechley made an e-textile construction kit that enables consumers to create their own soft interactive clothing. The patch shown here is actually a soft computer chip that functions as a stitchable Arduino, which can be sewn onto fabric.

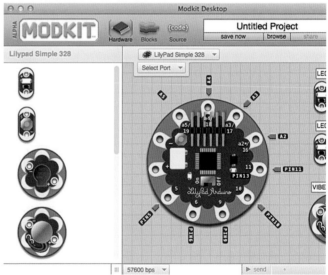

ABOVE / The LilyPad Arduino kit Buechley created is a set of sew-able electronic components that can be integrated into any garment. After buying the kit, consumers can use software called ModKit, created by High-Low Tech student Ed Baafi, that enables them to programme the components themselves.

LEFT / The LilyPad Arduino kit includes a range of electronic components, such as sensors, tiny speakers, switches, conductors and miniature LEDs. The Arduino component is linked to a computer by attaching an encapsulated FTDI cable to it.

BELOW LEFT & RIGHT / Here, the LilyPad Arduino kit is being used to make an interactive bag. The Lilypad is placed at the centre of the design where it sends electronic signals to the other components integrated into the fabric.

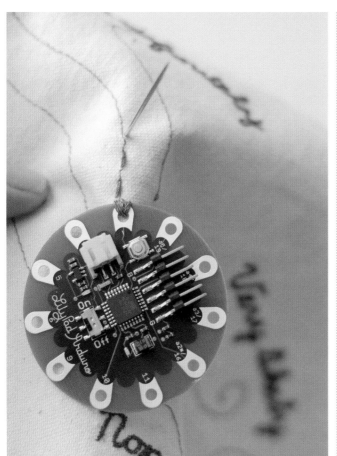

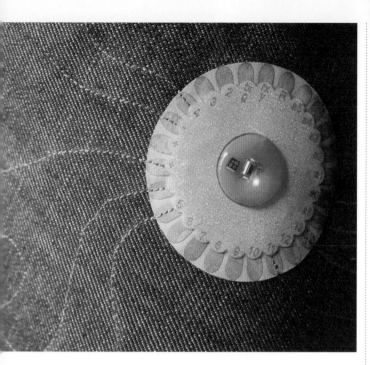

Buechley takes a grass roots approach to high-tech textiles, transforming them into intelligent devices that almost anyone can relate to, and even make themselves.

**LEFT & OPPOSITE PAGE,
BOTTOM** / Buechley's methods of
endowing textiles with electronics
and digital technology can be applied
to many other types of surfaces.
Conductive materials enable interior
lighting to be integrated into the Living
Wall wallpaper, which is activated by
touch alone.

**OPPOSITE PAGE, TOP LEFT & TOP
RIGHT** / Making electronic components
that are pliable and soft makes them
more compatible with textiles. Soft
circuitry and conductive threads
have proven to be just as effective as
hardware circuitry and conventional
wiring. Buechley is finding new ways
to make them appear stylish and chic.

RIGHT / The materials, colours, surface textures and structures McRae invents are intended to be both provocative and beautiful. They transform the body into sculptural shapes that seem more alien than human. This image is from 'Grow on You', created in collaboration with Bart Hess (Lucyandbart).

OPPOSITE / McRae crafts wearable structures. This honeycomb-like textile mesh moves with the wearer as clothing would. It is called 'Transnatural', and is made from the thermoplastic used on patients for MRI scanning.

LUCY McRAE

Australian born Lucy McRae is an artist and designer whose works reconfigure the shape of the human body. Taking the human form as her starting point, McRae designs wearable structures that dramatically transform the body's natural silhouette, and create coatings that resurface the skin. The textures, colours, motifs and embellishments McRae invents are as provocative as they are beautiful, and they morph the body into sculptural forms that seem more alien than human.

McRae's uncanny approach to fashion and her unique ability to redesign the human body are easy to see, but difficult to explain. When asked what her professional credentials are, McRae says simply that she is a 'body architect', and uses terms such as building, inventing and experimenting to describe her work. By using textiles and other fibre-based forms, or substances such as foam, feathers, paper and wood, McRae crafts wearable structures for the body to inhabit, which move with the wearer as clothing would.

At first, the elaborate designs that McRae creates appear to blur the boundaries between clothing and architecture, but many are expressions of body modification more than

they are garments that can be worn. 'Future fashion designers are likely to promote genetic manipulation techniques as a means of styling the body, or work with medical researchers to create prosthetic implants that radically alter the body's shape,' McRae explains. She is interested in provoking a redefinition of the role of the skin: her edible parfum being a good example, allowing the skin to perform as an atomiser, working from the inside out. McRae has been interested in body manipulation ever since she worked on Philips Design's Electronic Tattoo project, which explored the extent to which sensing technology could be embedded beneath the skin. 'At Philips we discovered that people are embracing wearable interactive technology,' McRae says. 'Even to the extent that some would consider having implants to manipulate their body shape or create temporary changes in their skin.'

The futuristic human archetypes that McRae creates have attracted the attention of the music industry, sparking commissions for extravagant performance costumes that transform pop stars into otherworldly creatures. Swedish pop star Robyn famously commissioned McRae to design and style her appearance for three of her album covers, and to create the performance costumes she wore in her 'Indestructible' video. 'The designs for Robyn's music video were the culmination of more than two years' research into dynamic textile forms made from liquid, air and vapour,' McRae says. 'The textiles Robyn wore were crafted from 1.2 kilometres (3/4 mile) of transparent plumbers' tubing, which was knitted with fishing wire so that it would sit close to her body. The tubes were connected to industrial pumps that streamed hundreds of litres of glycerol throughout the tubes, coupled with air valves that released air intermittently between the surges of the liquid. The air valves sent surges of radiant colours through the tubes, but at different speeds, so that the textile would appear to be a living, breathing dynamic skin that traversed the body.'

From 2007 to 2009 McRae developed a number of projects in collaboration with Dutch designer Bart Hess, a former colleague at Philips Design. Both have extensive experience of textile design, yet it is their fascination with genetic manipulation and living, breathing fabric forms that inspires them the most. 'Our collaborative works touch upon themes like genetics and body modification,' McRae says, 'but it's not our intention to try to take them forward. Bart and I worked in an instinctual way, sharing a mutual vision for creating new skins and future human shapes. We are blindly discovering low-tech prosthetics for human enhancement, which we feel is the way forward.'

ABOVE & LEFT / McRae's collaborative works with Bart Hess reference themes such as genetic manipulation and body modification. The two designers work together to create new skins and alternative body shapes. The 'Dripping Colour' prototypes shown here render a vision of how the body would look if it secreted beads of coloured sweat that crystallized on the skin. The top image is a still from a film McRae made about chlorophyll skin, experimenting with colour, movement and absorption.

OPPOSITE / Many of McRae's designs blur the boundaries between clothing and architecture. This garment, created in collaboration with Bart Hess, replaces fashion fabric with a hard substrate that explodes when the wearer is ready to remove it.

LEFT / Together, McRae and Hess share a vision for a human body that can be genetically engineered to grow alternative skins, sprout new surface textures or transform into new shapes. This design explores what such a body would look like on day one of germination.

BELOW / As the prototype of the genetically engineered design shown left continues to evolve, it would assume new forms and grow new surface textures. This design presents McRae and Hess's vision of how far it could evolve after one week of germination.

BELOW, LEFT & RIGHT / McRae replaces textiles with other fibre-based forms, or objects such as feathers, paper and wood. Here, elaborate skins have been created by lining the surface of the body with unusual materials. Each masks the wearer's identity, creating a future vision of how camouflage could be created. On the left is a Lucyandbart collaboration, on the right is Lucy's own creation.

By using textiles and other substances such as foam, feathers, paper and wood, Lucy McRae crafts wearable structures for the body to inhabit, which move with the wearer as clothing would.

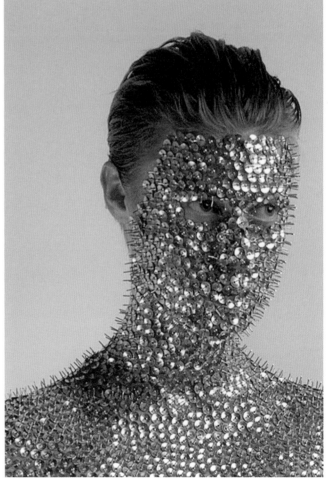

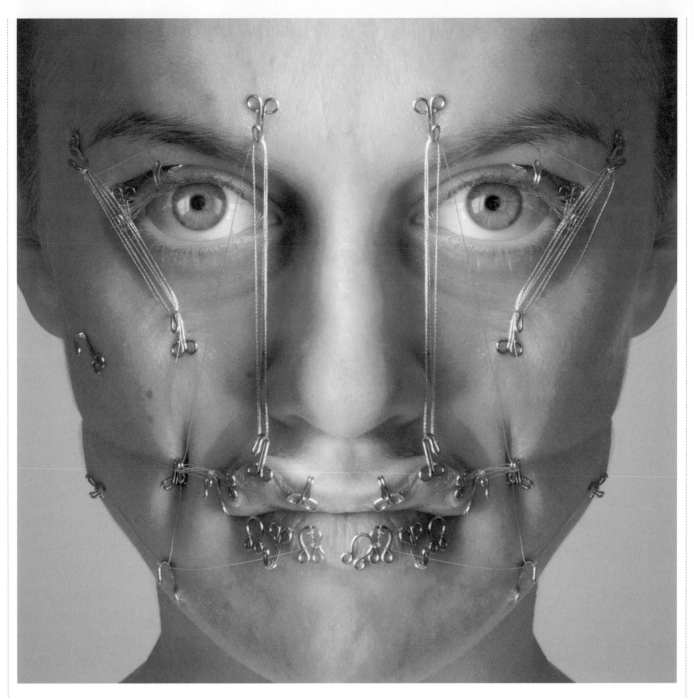

ABOVE / Cosmetic surgery is an invasive procedure that uses threads, implants and filaments to sculpt the body from within. This image, 'Hooks and Eyes', by Lucyandbart, shows how the appearance of the face can be manipulated on the skin as if the surgical procedures had been carried out on the surface itself rather than underneath it.

RIGHT / McRae and Hess foresee a time when genetic manipulation techniques will become a means of styling the body. Medical research and textile design could come together to create temporary changes in the skin.

BOTTOM LEFT / McRae is exploring what she describes as 'lo-tech prosthetics for human enhancement' by using ordinary materials to manipulate the body's shape and facial features.

BOTTOM RIGHT / Rather than dress the body in fabric, McRae and Hess are exploring the potential to create soft, formless surfaces that constantly reconfigure. This is from the series 'Grow on You'.

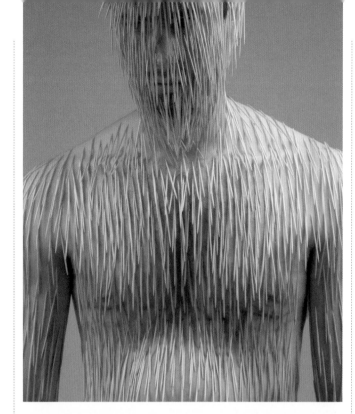

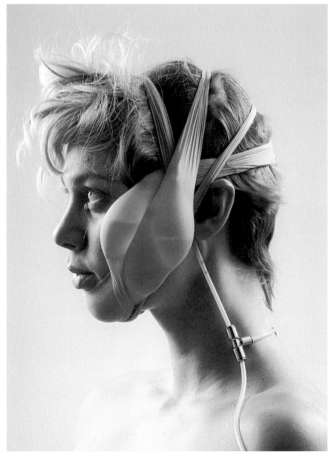

MAGGIE ORTH

One of the first practitioners to develop interactive textiles, Maggie Orth spent much of the 1990s in a science lab, looking for ways to incorporate electronics and conductive fibres into fabric. While carrying out her PhD research at the Massachusetts Institute of Technology (MIT) Media Lab, Orth invented wearable computer interfaces, electronic fabrics and musical instruments crafted from electronic parts and soft textile components. Orth obtained patents for her research projects, and then set up her own lab when she graduated from MIT.

Today, Orth is director of International Fashion Machines, the Seattle-based company she founded to develop new technologies and pioneer electronic textiles. International Fashion Machines use traditional textile practices to create electronic textiles. By finding contemporary expressions of traditional practices such as weaving and sewing, and integrating them with conductive yarns and traditional electronics, Orth and her colleagues create fabrics that can change colour, transmit light and sense touch. The fabrics and technologies that result have found expression in interactive dresses, animated fashion logos and tactile dimmer switches for lighting.

In addition to her design projects, Orth is also a practising artist. Textiles are her preferred media for both art and design. She says: 'Textiles enable me to handcraft my computational medium, creating circuits and electrical properties simultaneously with aesthetic design.' As she creates textile artworks and engineers fabrics for design applications, Orth gleans new insights into textile practice. 'Electronic textiles juxtapose two seemingly antithetical worlds,' she says. 'Fabrics, which are stereotyped as handcrafted, decorative and feminine, and computer technology, which is seen as mass-produced, functional and masculine. Choosing textiles as a medium allows me to physically transform technology from hard, functional and mass-produced into something soft, sensual and intimate.'

Although Orth's electronic textiles are precisely engineered to perform, there is an element of serendipity in the design process. Orth's colour-change textiles are typically woven with resistive yarns, then printed with thermochromic inks, which are dark and unsaturated when off, and brightly coloured when on. When electronics send an electric current to resistive yarns, the fabric heats up and changes colour. During the printing process, Orth can only estimate which colour changes will occur when she connects the circuit to the thermochromic printed areas. It isn't until the piece is programmed that Orth is able to gauge how the weave structure and pattern will interact with the thermochromic inks and see the shape and texture of the colour changes. Orth explains, 'My colour-change textiles are crafted in layers of woven fibres, printed inks and hidden circuitry. At the press of a button, viewers can begin to see how saturated colour, hidden electrical elements and woven structures interact, and enjoy the patterns that are revealed.'

Orth's experiments with conductive circuits reveal hidden relationships between electronic textiles and the human body. Her light-emitting work *Petal Pusher* combines textile touch sensors and transmissive fabric. When the viewer touches the textile sensor, a small electrical charge travels from the textile, through the body to the ground. 'The electrical nature of our bodies enables us to interact with conductive textiles,' Orth explains. 'Electronics react to the change in charge and cause the lights to dim or adjust, which reveals colours and patterns in the textiles.' Users can create immediate changes by touching the lofted sensors, and create new patterns by turning multiple units on and off. *Petal Pusher*'s combination of integrated lighting and soft textile sensors makes the experience of triggering electronic systems tactile and inviting.

Orth's works are high-tech, yet created with a broad range of textile processes, including machine embroidery, hand-tufting and woven pile, each of which creates different tactile effects. Orth's tactile works bridge the gap between the tactility of the fingertips and the rigid, uninviting surfaces characteristic of the technological world.

'Electronic textiles allow me to bring technology into the service of the creative and sensual,' Orth says. 'It reflects my belief that making and experiencing aesthetic and beautiful objects is an essential part of the human experience.'

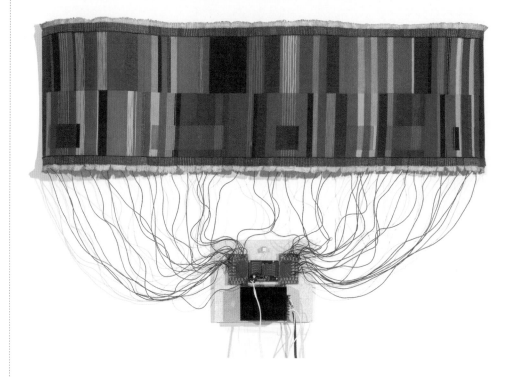

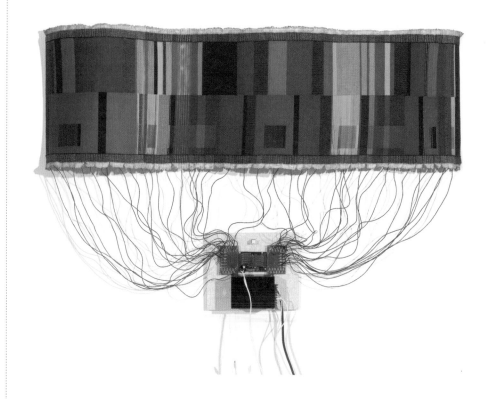

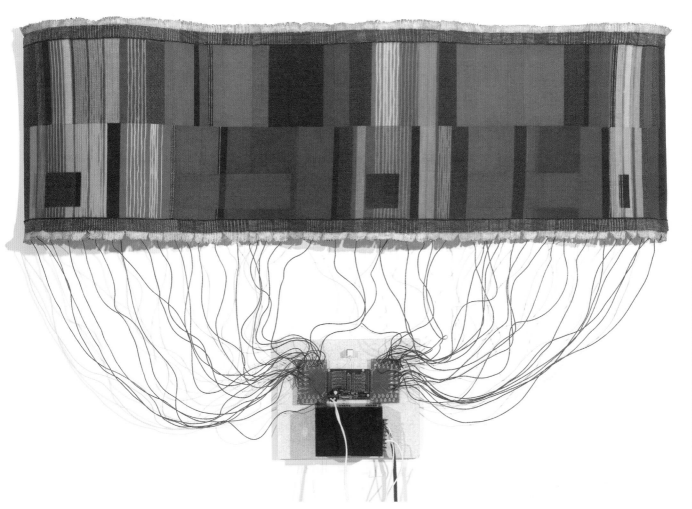

OPPOSITE, TOP / *100 Electronic Art Years* features different patterns and colour groupings. The artwork is interactive, enabling the viewer to move to different cycles by pushing a button. Cycles are determined by colour coding and whether odd or even numbers have been assigned to the groupings of fibres. In the cycle here, only the colours that have been assigned even numbers are highlighted.

OPPOSITE, BOTTOM / The artwork is mounted to the wall on a curved support, with wires and electronics intentionally revealed. In this cycle, the artwork highlights only green and yellow fibres.

ABOVE / Orth wove the artwork by hand, creating 50 textile pixels. It is woven on black-and-white double weave. Only the colours assigned odd numbers are highlighted in this cycle.

RIGHT / As with all colour-change textiles, the colours will eventually burn out and stop changing, leaving permanent colours on the surface. Once that happens, Orth says, the artwork can be considered complete.

Maggie Orth's textiles combine high-tech performance with soft textures created by embroidery, hand-tufting and woven pile, making them irresistibly tactile.

BOTTOM LEFT / Shown here in its yellow phase, *Barcodeman*'s software has activated all pixels with yellow colour in them and turned off the pixels containing other colours. Motifs woven into the horizontal band of fibres are beginning to appear.

BOTTOM RIGHT / When shifting to its pink and red phase, shown here, yarns integrated into the back layer of *Barcodeman*'s double-weave structure are slowly heated to make the phase change more subtle.

THIS PAGE / *BLIP* is one of the seven electronic pieces made for Orth's Moving Toward Stillness series. The artwork is programmed to change colour over time, and finally burn a lasting colour into the surface. *BLIP* is crafted from hand-woven cotton, conductive yarns, silver ink, silk-screen ink, thermochromic ink, drive electronics, electrical parts and expressive software.

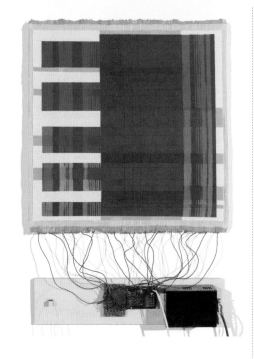

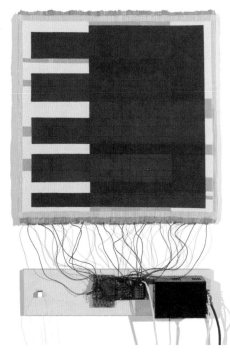

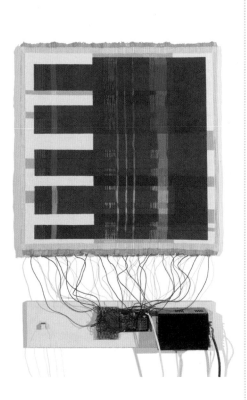

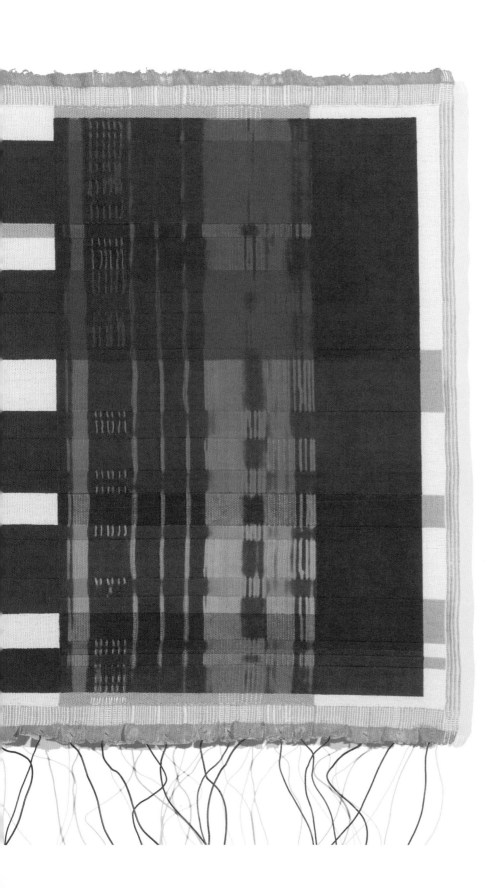

LEFT / As the title suggests, *BLIP* was created to cause a momentary change within an area of stillness, bringing colour, action and motion to a surface that is otherwise still. The artwork contains 16 colour pixels printed on a grey-and-white double weave. Yarns and conductive threads are bundled together to create surface texture.

NANCY TILBURY

Since establishing her fashion lab in 2009, Nancy Tilbury has pioneered an impressive range of highly imaginative and technologically advanced designs. An expert on new media and high-tech materials, Tilbury creates smart fabrics for custom-made garments, sportswear designs and street-wear brands. Tilbury takes a sci-fi view of the fabrics of the future, and together with collaborators, finds fashion applications for advanced technology and scientific research. 'Our focus is digital and physical intimacy,' says Tilbury. 'We use digital systems to create synergy between the body and its surroundings. We use wearable technology to amplify the body's physical space, making the experience of wearing clothing more dynamic.'

Tilbury typically combines her expertise with that of specialists from disciplines other than fashion and textiles. 'My projects are developed in collaboration with engineers, scientists, stylists and technology developers,' Tilbury explains. 'We bring smart fabrics to market as well as creating ways that fashion brands can use science and technology to reposition themselves.' Tilbury cites the example of her Fashion Phreaking project, in which she used denim fabric as a substrate for an interactive jeans jacket that could be triggered to light up. 'The jacket integrates playful technologies, conductive textile networks and soft switching into denim fabric', Tilbury explains. 'I call the technique "denim disruption" as it transforms denim into a digital skin that expands the wearer's ability to

BELOW / Tilbury's Body Atmosphere research project looks at how intangible forms can form garments on the body. The study for the Cloud Gown, shown here, is essentially a cloud of particles that will begin to assemble into a garment when it comes into contact with the wearer's body.

OPPOSITE PAGE, ABOVE & RIGHT / Tilbury is exploring the extent to which textiles could be programmed to create chameleon-like skins. Her Digital Skins series looks at the potential to make garments that could be altered to create colourful skins, or engineered to make the wearer merge into the background.

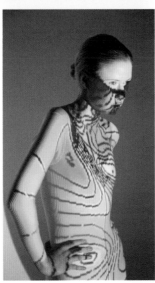

communicate by projecting light. It disrupts the viewer's normal understanding of how denim, or potentially any other high-street fashion fabric, is supposed to perform.'

In addition to bringing smart fabrics, such as the Levi's Philips ICD+ line in the late 90s, to market, and creating fashion prototypes for the high street, Tilbury also designs performance costumes for the film and music industries. Tilbury is one of the founders of Studio XO, who famously created technologically enhanced stage costumes for the musical group Black Eyed Peas' 2011 world tour. Commissioned jointly by Philips Lighting and fashion stylist B. Åkerlund, the garments were crafted with integrated communication technology that enabled them to engage with wireless systems on and around the stage. Sensors and soft circuit controls triggered video projections, initiated light shows and signalled audio loops to play. LEDs integrated into the fabrics created moving motifs and enabled their surfaces to pulsate and change colour. The costumes are described as larger than life, which makes sense, considering that they were created to project and amplify the movements choreographed by big personalities on stage.

Although Tilbury's current output is anchored to textile substrates and physical garments, she foresees a time when clothing can be an ephemeral experience. Inspired by biological engineering, new developments in nanotechnology and the concept of self-assembly,

Tilbury introduced a collection of designs created without cloth or conventional fabrication methods. 'Clothing could become biologically engineered, and line the body without using a single textile,' Tilbury says. 'Garments could be formed by gases and nanoelectronic particles that automatically assemble on the body. Certain types of liquids could be engineered to thicken as they are applied to the body and form "second skin" fashions. If you consider what I call "swallowable technologies", which will be tablets or nano-probes that spark changes on the skin from within the body, fashion fabric could be replaced by patterns that emerge on the skin, causing colour changes or temporary textures. I am anticipating a time when couture will be cultivated from within the body, and second skin garments will be formed by particles that automatically assemble on human flesh.'

The radical designs Tilbury anticipates will create garments without using a single textile, indicating that fashion fabrics may transform dramatically in future, or even become redundant. 'I believe that technology is enabling fashion design to move closer to a magical interdisciplinary area where anything is possible,' Tilbury says. 'Intimate sensing and even physical adaptations applied to fabrics would allow the look and feel of our clothing to be reconfigured. Our relationship to clothing and cloth, its function, meaning and emotional content will transform our understanding of fashion textiles as we know them today.'

ABOVE & RIGHT / Tilbury foresees a day when the human body will be genetically engineered to 'grow' fashion and accessories that literally are a second skin. Tilbury's Flesh Dress, shown here, shows how the body would look if it could grow cloth-like membranes in order to clothe itself.

OPPOSITE PAGE / Textiles are already beginning to be made in fluid form. Some can be sprayed onto the body to form a textile as they dry, and Tilbury believes that in future some fashion textiles will be applied to the body like lotion. Tilbury's Bespoke Fluo Dress is shown here.

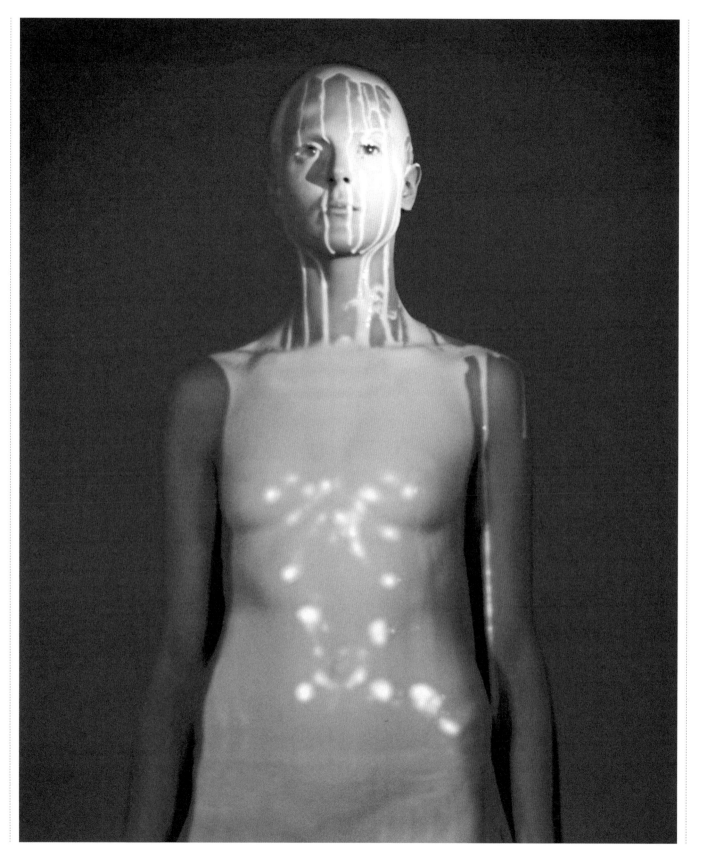

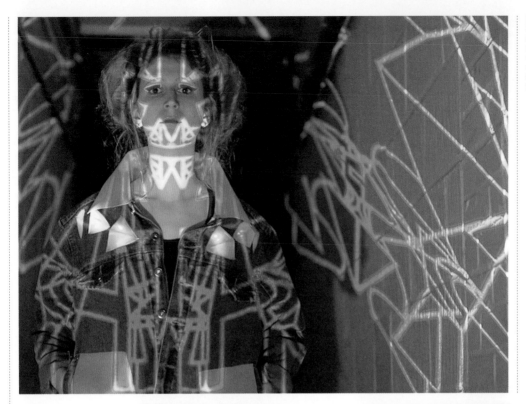

LEFT & BELOW / Tilbury set up the Fashion Phreaking initiative to give smart clothing and intelligent fabric a new context. By applying conductive textile networks and soft switching to denim garments, Tilbury creates digital skins designed to make smart clothing more playful.

ABOVE / The Spike Jacket was designed to amplify the wearer's perception of personal space. Sensors integrated into the jacket detect when others come too close, triggering a system of textile cabling and silicone light diffusers to flash. The jacket lets those around the wearer know to keep their distance.

LEFT / The renderings shown here depict Tilbury's vision of how the body, technology and genetic engineering can come together as one. Here, an artificial heel emerges from the foot, replacing the need for high-heeled shoes.

BELOW LEFT / In Tilbury's vision for the merger of technology and flesh, an electronic cream she calls e-Pannosa could be applied to the skin to transform it. Substances in the cream would interface with the body's natural conductors to create changes on the surface of the skin.

BELOW / Tilbury shows what a flesh ring could look like if it could be 'grown' by the body rather than simply put on and worn.

Tilbury foresees a day when garments will be created without using a single textile, indicating that fashion fabrics may become redundant.

SABINE SEYMOUR

Sabine Seymour first encountered technology as a child, when she was given a Commodore 64 computer by her father. As a teenager, she taught herself to programme computers and had designed her own clothes. When she finished her education, Seymour brought the two interests together in a series of technologically enhanced garments, and established Moondial, a fashion technology lab with studios in Austria and New York, where prototypes or products are created as Moondial with specialists or consortium partners. Seymour is currently establishing a 'fashionable technology' lab at Parsons The New School for Design in New York, where smart fabrics and information technology will come together in wearable designs.

Seymour never set out to work specifically with textiles, but pondering the points where clothing and technology could come together sparked her interest in smart fabrics. Today, exploring the potentials that nanotechnology has for smart textiles, designing electronic fabrics and wearable/mobile applications, and creating new manufacturing and finishing processes is a significant part of Seymour's research and an essential part of the Moondial Lab's exploration. 'Technologized textiles can be a second skin, and function as things we wear, carry or attach to our bodies,' Seymour says. 'They can also facilitate the interactions between our body and other networks, and interact with the space that surrounds us and the people we meet.'

One of Moondial's dynamic design prototypes is the 'View Jacket', which features an embedded Lumalive display made by Philips Design. The display can project pictures, moving images, scrolling texts and morphing patterns, transforming the jacket into an animated surface. 'The design of the jacket is contextualized for specific events,' Seymour explains. 'The dynamic movement on the surface draws attention. It could be programmed to broadcast brand logos or advertising slogans, which would make it a great tool for guerrilla marketing. Programmed with patterns, images or animations that the wearer likes, it can become a fashion statement.' Seymour plans to fully integrate the digital display and technological components in future versions of the design. 'The goal is to enhance the fibres so that the display potential is built into them as they are manufactured, rather than adding electronics to them after they have been woven into fabric.'

Transforming static fabrics into dynamic surfaces seems to be a hallmark of Seymour's work as she endows other types of garments with the potential to change motifs. Her light-reactive 'Sun' T shirt, for example, uses simple UV light to morph the graphics printed on the front into shapes. 'The shirt functions as a canvas to tell a story,' Seymour says, 'and the sun provides the switch that turns on the graphics and enables them to reveal new images. The T shirt harvests UV light to create a self-contained power source, making it an example of sustainability. Seymour's T shirt 'Sun N°01 Zebra' was produced in a limited edition and launched at The Ars

ABOVE / Seymour takes an innovative approach to technology and materials: she lists sunlight among the materials used to make this zebra-print T-shirt, as UV light is required to make the zebra's head appear on the surface.

Electronica Festival in 2009, and is now considered to be a collector's item.

Seymour is setting new standards for manufacturing. As she sources new materials, develops novel techniques and creates supply chains that streamline the production of wearable technology, she faces industry limitations head on. 'Because wearable technology is still a new area, designers are faced with issues that need to resolved before techno textiles and wearables can move forward,' Seymour explains. 'IP-related issues, venture capital investment and specialist manufacturing can restrict designers.' She also believes that consumers can play a role in the process: 'Some

consumers would like to self-assemble wearable garments and techno textiles,' she says. 'Customized 3D printing or on-the-fly knitting could be made a part of the retail experience. I think the pairing of a gallery-like store with an Apple-style genius bar would enable consumers to customize wearable technology, making it simpler to buy and easier to use.'

Seymour's research into wearable technologies is producing fresh concepts and sparking new ideas about the fashion textiles of the future. Her pioneering work is part of a global network that is setting new standards for smart textiles, and the industry in general.

LEFT & ABOVE / The Sun Nº05 Scarf, shown here, needs UV light to make the motif visible. The sun changes the surface from static to dynamic as, without it, the motif becomes invisible.

BELOW / The moon is depicted against a black background in the Sun Nº02 Moon T-shirt. Sunlight enables the moon to change colour, ranging from soft pink to hot pink as the sunlight becomes stronger.

OPPOSITE PAGE / Like the Sun scarf, the Sun Nº04 Girls T-shirt uses UV light to create changes on the surface. Sunlight triggers soft pink colours to appear in the illustration, which grow in intensity when the sunlight gets stronger.

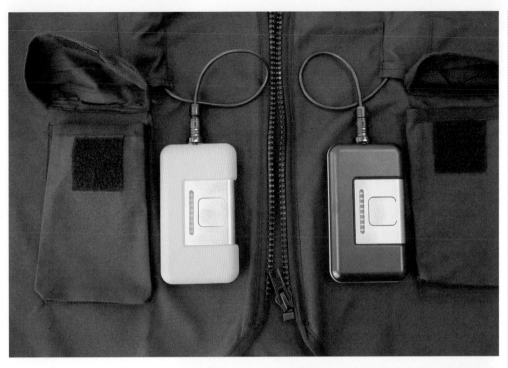

Sabine Seymour is pioneering second skins that facilitate interactions between the body and the technological systems around them, and create networks between individuals.

ABOVE & RIGHT / These close-ups are of Seymour's Funcl Demo Jackets, prototype garments designed to be worn in the aftermath of a large-scale disaster. The garments include lighting, GPS technology and gas detectors that can help the wearers to find safety.

BOTTOM / This version of the Funcl Demo Jacket is equipped with sensors that detect poisonous emissions. In the aftermath of a disaster, identifying and monitoring gas leaks could save lives.

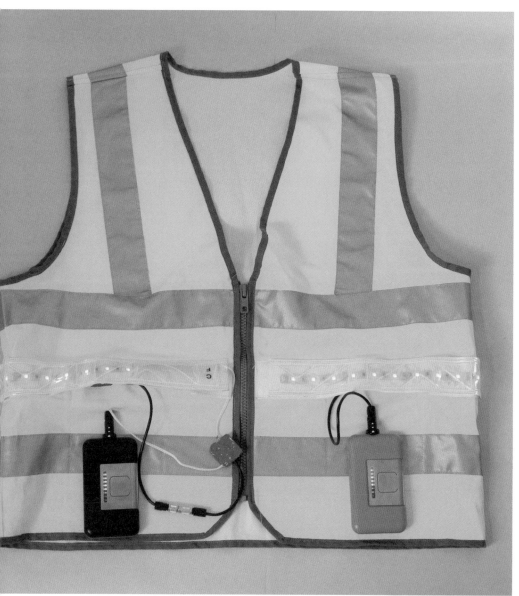

RIGHT / The LEDs embedded in the garment are visible in both darkness and daylight. The LEDs are able to pulsate or remain static, and can change colour if needed. Because LEDs do not emit heat it is safe to wear them against the body for long periods.

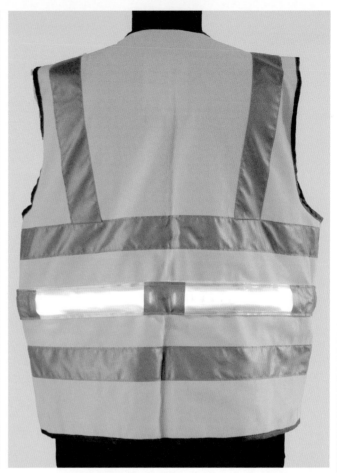

ABOVE & RIGHT / The prototypes from the Funcl Demo Display Vo1 project shown here make active lighting, GPS location devices and gas detectors wearable. The project was originally a commission from a government agency, which Moondial developed with consortium partners.

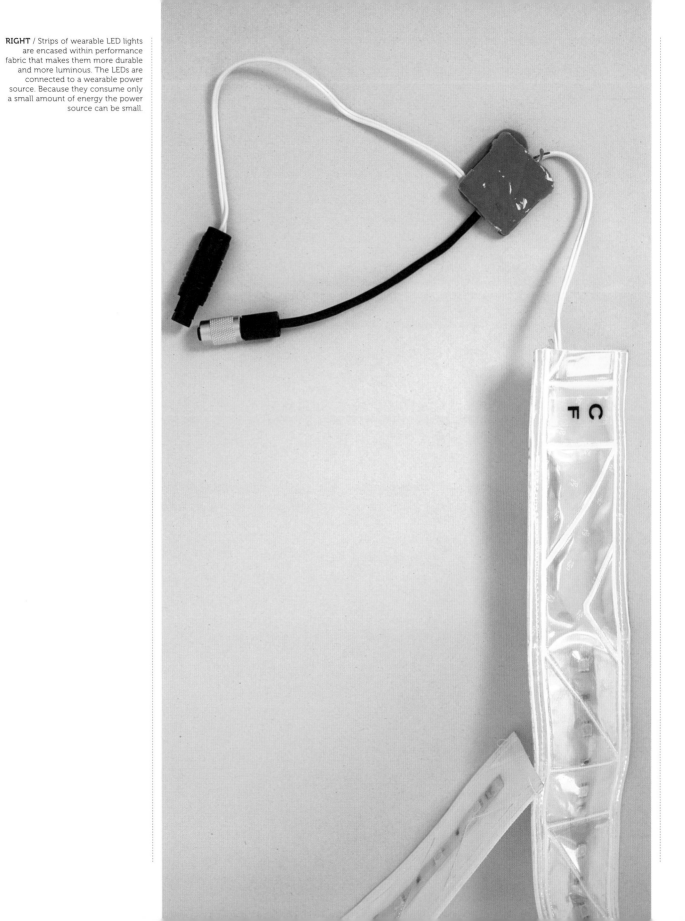

RIGHT / Strips of wearable LED lights are encased within performance fabric that makes them more durable and more luminous. The LEDs are connected to a wearable power source. Because they consume only a small amount of energy the power source can be small.

LEFT & BELOW LEFT / The View N°01 jackets shown here are made with animated display screens embedded on the surface. Not only can these prototypes be worn by sports fans to show their loyalty to the team, the digital screens even enable them to keep score.

BELOW / The View N°03 jacket uses Lumalive by Philips to make the display screen on the sleeve move and pulsate. Designed to look like a baseball jacket, it can be worn by fans and triggered to blink and pulsate to cheer on the team.

OPPOSITE PAGE / The View N°02 jacket, shown here, is a trendy urban design with a flexible display screen embedded into the back. Emblazoned with embroidered patches, the display screen can also be programmed to project messages in support of sports teams and other organizations.

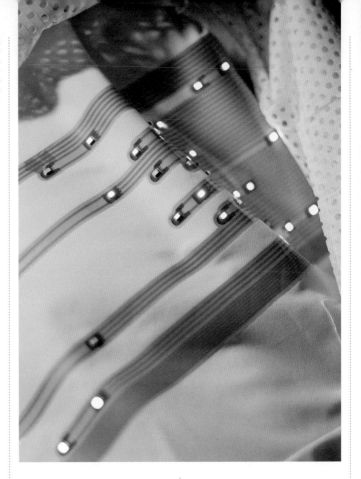

STRETCHABLE CIRCUITS

When microsystems technologist Christian Dils, microelectronics engineer René Vieroth, physicist Thomas Loeher and medical engineer Manuel Seckel joined forces to pool their technological expertise, they set a new standard for wearable technology. Based in Berlin, at technology research institute Fraunhofer IZM, the start-up they established is called Stretchable Circuits, named after the flexible, stretchable electronic systems they integrate into fashion fabrics, and adapt for textiles produced for industrial applications. As Stretchable Circuits make it possible to integrate electronic components and technological systems into textiles, they are dramatically advancing the emerging fields of wearable technology and smart textiles. Stretchable Circuits' clients and collaborators include fashion designers and industrial partners keen to incorporate technology into a wide range of textile-based objects. Stretchable Circuit's soft textile circuitry has been included in products made for interior design, lightweight lighting systems and even automotive parts.

Whereas others active in the field attach technological parts to substrates, Stretchable Circuits actually create stretchable electronic systems, which they laminate to fabrics. 'We do not have weaving or knitting expertise at Stretchable Circuits, so we source base fabrics we can laminate our systems onto,' explains Christian Dils. 'We rely mostly on textile research labs

RIGHT / The Cyber Nomade Suit, shown here, was created to explore how a 'utopian' textile would function. Stretchable Circuits designed a wearable fabric that could create a digital display, or create chameleon-like changes in the outer surface.

OPPOSITE / Stretchable Circuits teamed up with the German textile developer Novanex to create an interactive system for performance costumes made from soft, stretchable substrates. The result was a 'toolkit' set of programmable components that could easily be integrated into clothing.

to provide us with conductive materials, ribbons and substrates.' For some applications, Stretchable Circuits use the stretchable circuit board they make from thermoplastic elastomeric foil and copper as a base material, onto which they solder miniaturized electronic modules. For others, organic materials are the textiles of choice. 'We've experimented with laminating the stretchable circuit boards onto different kinds of textile materials like denim, cotton, silk and leather,' explains Dils, 'and always got good results'.

Stretchable Circuits investigate fresh approaches to creating electronic textiles, using new methods of embroidering with conductive yarn, crimping isolated textile wires and

integrating circuits into fabrics developed by Fraunhofer IZM. The key to making technologized fabrics operable is the miniaturization of the electronic parts, and Stretchable Circuits' microelectronic units are small and lightweight enough to coat the fabric's surface. They have also designed micro-embedded LED circuits that can be transferred by heat into garments, programmed with a range of performances and cleaned in a washing machine like most other textiles.

Stretchable Circuits have strong ties with the Technical University of Berlin, where they supervise labs and hold workshops. They teach students how to integrate electronic parts into textile substrates, use conductive yarns to create simple circuits and write

programming codes. Projects at Berlin University of the Arts resulted in groundbreaking interactive garments, and collaborations with Austrian fashion designer Wolfgang Langeder transformed lighting technology into wearable chic. 'We like the interdisciplinary nature of the field we work in,' says Dils. 'I believe engineers and designers benefit from collaborating with each other and sharing new technologies and materials. Unless we find good design applications for our technologies, our work will not see the light of day.'

In recent years, lighting has become a primary research interest for Stretchable Circuits. A demand for integrating soft-circuit lights into fashion, interior design and automobiles has motivated Stretchable Circuits to advance integrated lighting to the point where it can be considered one of the most stable interactive technologies. 'One of our current projects is developing a new kind of smart RGB (red-green-blue) LED pixels for wearable digital displays,' Dils explains. 'Yet, at the same time, we make use of the advances occurring in flexible substrate technologies such as foils, stretchables and fabrics.' Stretchable Circuits plan to use the technology to make lighting products, such as lamps that are not fixed to the ceiling, but integrated into the surrounding surfaces. Curtains that illuminate when closed to mimic daylight are also on the drawing board, as are medical bandages that shine light on the body to treat skin conditions.

As Stretchable Circuits continue to pioneer new types of flexible and stretchable electronic systems, they promise to break new ground in fashion, interior textiles, medical applications and lighting. By branching out into new areas, such as medical research, Stretchable Circuits are finding fresh applications for electronic systems. 'We're embarking on research projects to create robotic skins, wearable keyboards and sensor-based textiles that detect the presence of a human,' Dils says. 'Human needs are the motivation for everything we do, and creating textiles for use in the health, security and communications sectors helps us improve the quality of everyday life.'

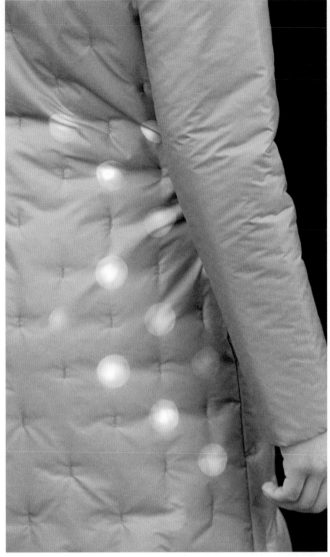

ABOVE LEFT & RIGHT / The garment shown here is part of the Disappear wearable technology project led by Theresa Lusser. In consultation with Stretchable Circuits, the designer created a coat that illuminates in response to the lights surrounding it, making the wearer blend in with the cityscape, appearing to 'disappear'.

Stretchable Circuits investigate fresh approaches to electronic textiles, creating soft fabric circuitry for use in apparel, architecture, lighting and even automotive parts.

ABOVE & LEFT / In collaboration with the Berlin-based fashion label Moon, Stretchable Circuits created light-emitting components that could be integrated into fabric. The design shown here, 'Klight' by Mareike Michel, reveals the edgy aesthetic many of the components had, which created dynamic light/shadow effects.

RIGHT / This dress by Moon Berlin is equipped with technology designed by Stretchable Circuits. Miniature electronic parts, tiny microelectronic units and micro-embedded LED circuits enable the garment to light up.

BELOW / The canvas light shown here is a flexible fabric light which can be easily adapted to suit different interior lighting requirements. The canvas was developed by Stephanie Horning as part of Berlin University of the Arts' Lichten project. Stretchable Circuits created the electrical layer, consisting of 256 white LEDs.

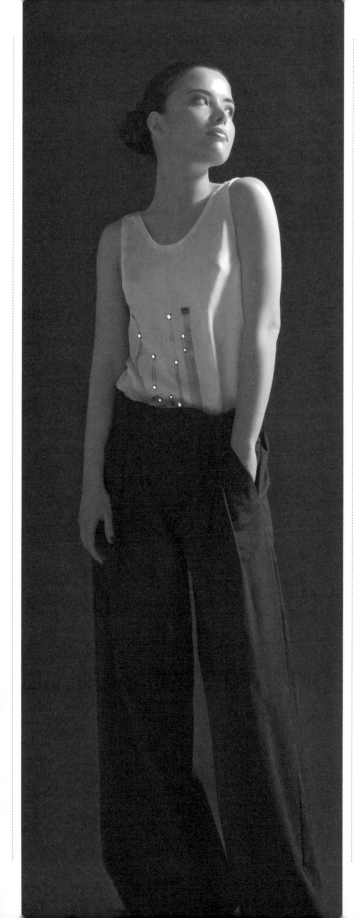

THIS PAGE / The demand for fabric with integrated lighting has been met by Stretchable Circuits, who have advanced the application of wearable LEDs dramatically in recent years. Garments like these contain integrated lighting so advanced that it is even washable. The white top on the left was created with MOON Berlin, while the dresses are part of a collaboration with Novanex.

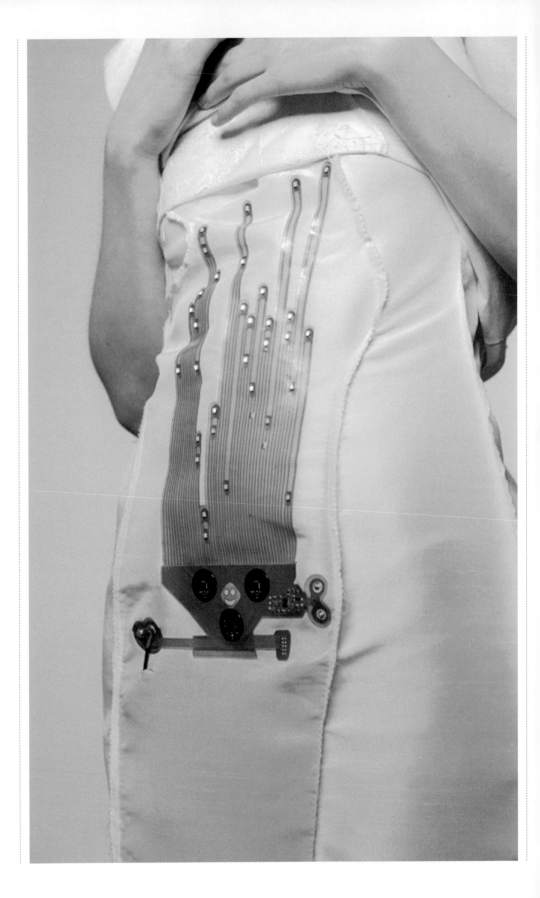

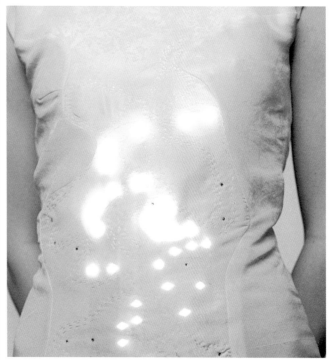

ABOVE & RIGHT / The Pneuma Dress, designed by Synne Frydenberg, was created to remind the wearer to breathe deeply. Stretchable Circuits integrated a respiration sensor into the fabric, which is connected to a microcontroller that makes inhalation and exhalation trigger LEDs to illuminate.

RIGHT / The Symmetrical Modern 001
Dress shown here is embedded with
LEDs that change in luminosity as
ambient light levels rise and fall.
The dress is printed with a graphic
pattern that traces the conductive
threads integrated into the fabric.

VALÉRIE LAMONTAGNE

Fascinated by technology's potential to create electronic interfaces between the body and the world around it, Canadian designer Valérie Lamontagne set out to create garments that merged machines, data, fibres and electronic parts. An artist, designer, theorist and digital media expert, Lamontagne uses her knowledge and crafts skills to make fibre-based electronic systems that are compatible with human needs. Her clothing designs are customizable, interactive, efficient and stylish, and so progressive in performance that they seem less like expressions of fibre-based technology, and more like blueprints for fashion's future.

Lamontagne set up a design lab in Montreal to integrate technology with fashion textiles. Called 3lectromode, Lamontagne's lab was the first of its kind in Canada. Working in tandem with a team of fashion and textile designers as well as programmers and engineers, Lamontagne operates within the field known as 'wearables'. 'We develop wearable technology intended to enrich everyday experiences by giving the wearers a new awareness of themselves and the world around them,' she says. 'Our work creates new connections between humans and the world of machines, information, environmental data and organic materials.'

Among the designs 3lectromode have brought to market are light-emitting garments and handbags that feature changing motifs. Their 'Asymmetrical' and 'Symmetrical Modern' dresses are made from cotton printed with minimalist patterns programmed to change shape in response to commands from technology integrated into the fabric. Embedded with LEDs, the dresses' levels of luminosity can be programmed to brighten when ambient lighting levels begin to fade. The Flower Bag is crafted in cotton, silk and leather, and made with integrated LEDs that respond to motion. The bags are customizable; consumers can choose from a selection of patterns and combine them in a variety of ways.

3lectromode recently introduced 'kit' versions of their garments that consumers can customize according to their own sense of style and technological specifications. Created with a DIY methodology in mind, each kit contains a garment and electronic parts ready for assembly. Electronic schematics and sewing directions are printed directly on the garments, stylishly integrating the assembly instructions into the fabric's motif. Like following a 'paint by numbers' methodology, the electronic components can be integrated into the design without recourse to an instruction manual. Each kit offers the means to create a customizable design, including different patterns to choose from. The range of parts includes electronic components such as LEDs, kinetics sensors, accelerometers and conductive threads. All are battery-operated and washable once the batteries are removed. 'The objective behind the kits is to create trendy DIY wearables that fuse fashion with electronics,' Lamontagne explains. 'We are creating a collection of designs and technological applications

which are easily fabricated by the consumer, taking the guesswork out of electronics assembly while creating a custom-made garment.'

With their fabric substrates, easy-assembly sensors and DIY ethos, 3lectromode's kits bridge the gap between textile design and electronic systems. While wearable technology may seem out of reach for some consumers, the kits' comprehensive assembly methods demystify the process. 'We want to make technology more accessible, because it heightens the wearer's social interactions as well as their sense of self-expression,' Lamontagne explains. 'A big part of our design ethos is creating a library of open-sourced tools, patterns and textile designs which can easily be used by anyone. We want to create a future where textile design and wearable technology are democratic and accessible.'

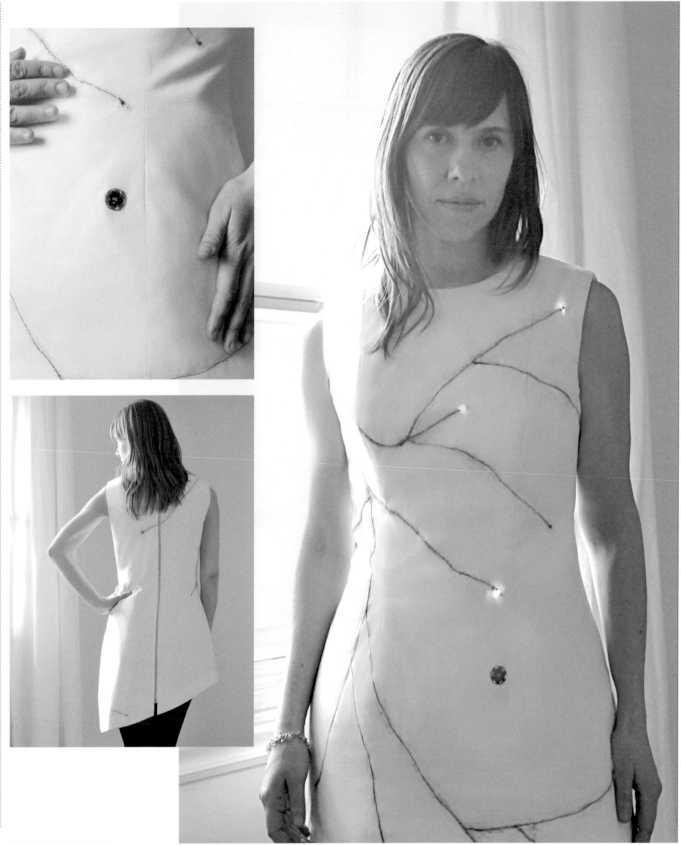

ABOVE LEFT & RIGHT /
Lamontagne sketched out the
Flower Shopping Bag's pattern
and shape by hand, then created
these digital versions of them.

RIGHT / The Flower Shopping Bag
is crafted in custom-printed cotton
and silk and made with integrated
LEDs that respond to motion.
Each bag is created from a kit that
contains a selection of patterns
which consumers are free
to combine in various ways.

OPPOSITE / The Asymmetrical
Modern Dress merges micro
machines, data, fibres and
electronic parts. The parts are
sold in a kit that the wearer can
assemble according to guidelines
or choose to customize to suit
individual style.

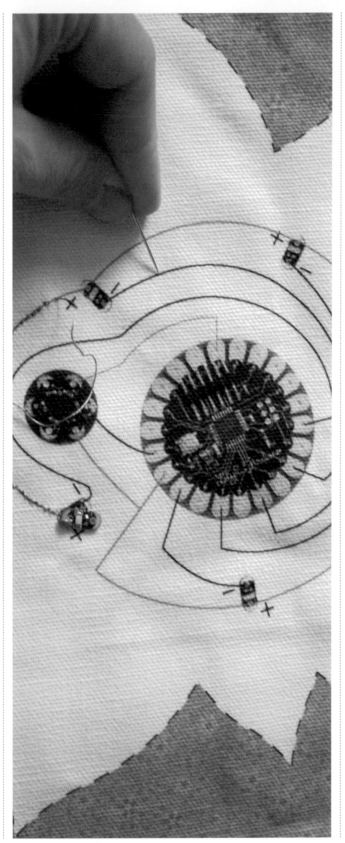

RIGHT / The Flower Shopping Bag is sold as a kit containing fabric and electronic parts ready for assembly. This part of the design contains motion sensors and LEDs that flicker as the bag moves.

LEFT / Schematics and step-by-step directions are printed directly on the fabric, making it easy to integrate the electronic parts into the design. The fabric shown here reveals where the pre-programmed LilyPad Arduino and LEDs should be sewn and connected by conductive thread.

Valérie Lamontagne creates garments that are so progressive in performance they seem less like expressions of fibre-based technology, and more like blueprints for fashion's future.

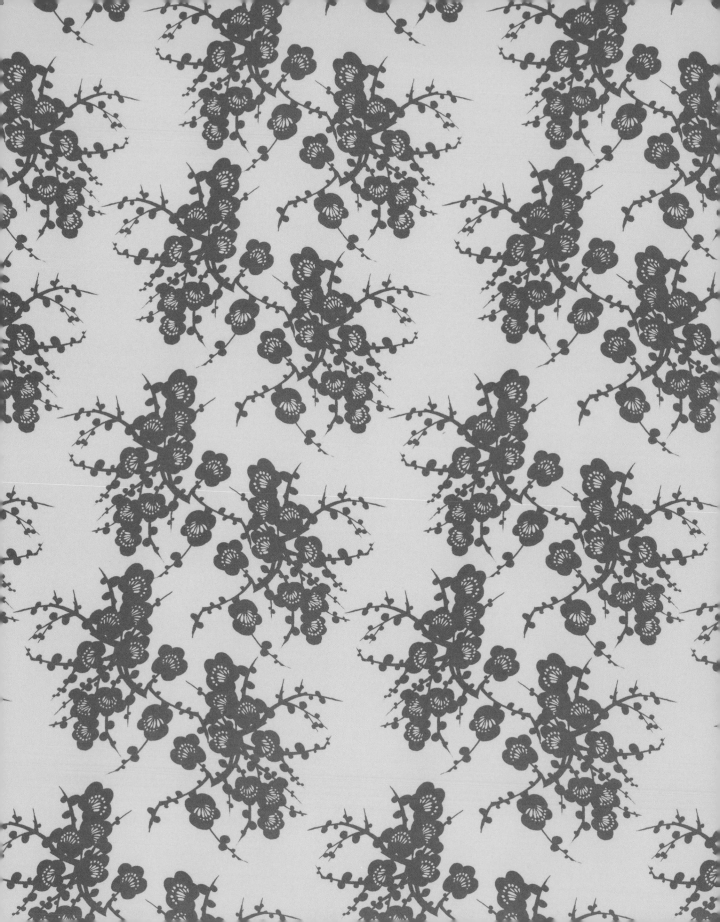

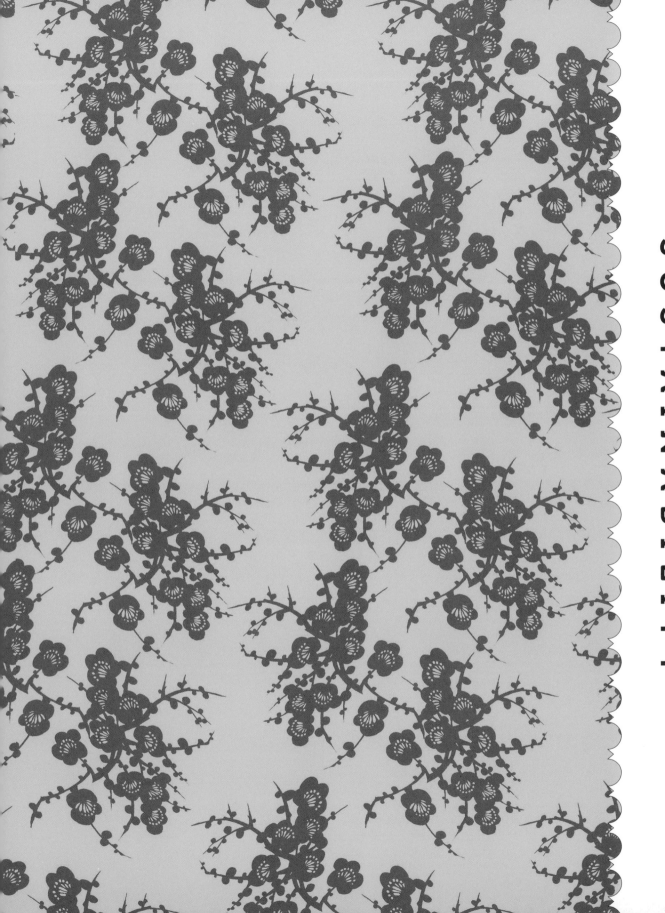

SUSTAINABILITY

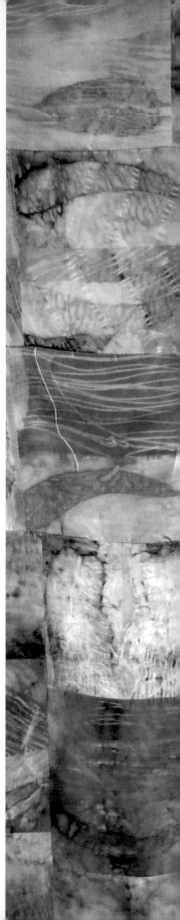

LEFT / The shift towards sustainability is inspiring designers to reconsider the inherent properties that natural fibres have. Like their manmade counterparts, natural fibres can be flame-retardant, water-resistant and highly resilient.

RIGHT, CENTRE / Designers such as India Flint are rediscovering the rich pigments found in nature. Heat processes, water quality and natural fixatives can be precisely engineered to harvest the colours of flowers and leaves and create a lasting print on fabric.

FAR RIGHT / Biodegradable fabrics can dissolve quickly and effortlessly, ending textile waste. Helen Storey envisions smart fabrics with a shelf life that will automatically disintegrate, while Emily Crane creates edible fabrics that can provide a source of nutrients.

AS DESIGNERS DEVELOP

new methods of constructing and consuming textiles, they are challenging traditional ideas about their use, function, life cycle and disposal. With sustainability in mind, designers find ways of enhancing the textiles they create to make them more durable and lengthen their lifespan. The growing movement to produce sustainable textiles is advocating a holistic, cradle-to-grave approach, which takes into account the impact of the textile's entire life cycle. As a result, new production methods are beginning to reduce the industry's carbon footprint, as well as the amount of textile waste that gets dumped in landfills all over the world.

Today's textile designers are interpreting sustainability in a variety of ways. For some, petitioning manufacturers to use organic materials and environmentally friendly processes enables them to work more responsibly. Many designers use recycled materials, while others prefer organic fabrics such as Ingeo, Cocona, hemp and raw silk. Biodegradable textiles, recycled plastics and renewable melt-processable fibres that can be woven into fabrics and/or made into non-woven textiles are also popular choices. Some designers develop socially responsible methods for fabric production, creating jobs for marginalized workers that boost local economies.

A handful of textile designers are forging alliances with science to create sustainable textiles, exploring the extent to which biochemistry can create new fabrics. Others look for natural know-how, exploring the insights into nature that researchers in biomimicry reveal. Biomimetic researchers identify processes used by animals, insects, plants and microbes to create materials and techniques that can significantly improve design.

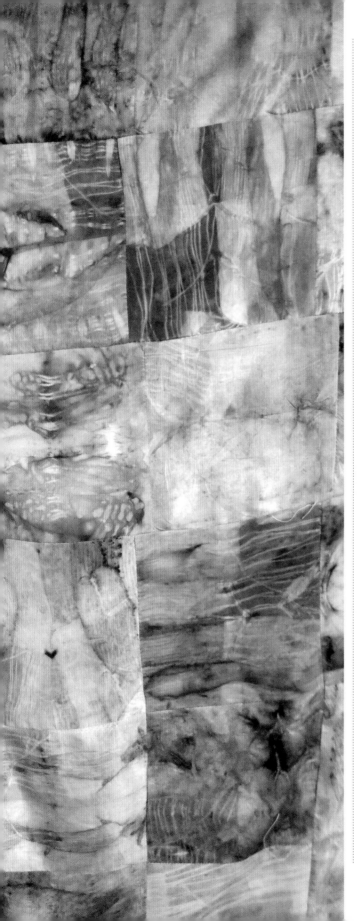

Plant fibres, pine cones and peacock quills have provided inspiration for new types of textiles, even leading designers to conceive of fabrics that 'grow' on the wearer's body.

Just as textile designers team up with technologists to engineer the fabrics of the future, some practitioners are joining forces with recycling initiatives to clean up consumer waste. Not all designers regard the production of new materials as a viable solution. Some tackle the growing problem of textile waste by devising methods for recycling the excess fabric that results from over-production. Others are finding ways to transform waste materials such as plastic into textiles that are as beautiful as they are sustainable, ensuring that the processes used to create them also reduce the risk of polluting waterways.

This section showcases 12 designers whose works reveal new ways of interpreting sustainability. Designers such as Margo Selby, Ptolemy Mann and Ismini Samanidou remain true to time-honoured techniques, and advocate the careful management of resources as a means of creating sustainable designs. Carole Collet and Veronika Kapsali have found inspiration in science-based research, while India Flint and Emily Crane use organic materials to create unique colours and textures. Whether crafted into chic clothing, stylish interior accessories or striking artworks, the sustainable forms showcased in this section reveal the beauty and innovation that sustainable approaches can yield.

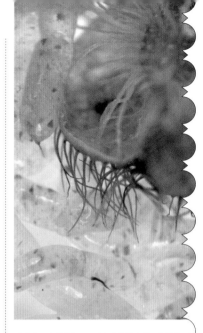

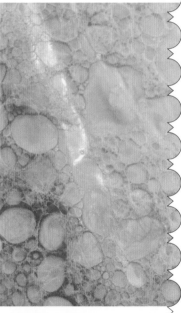

CAROLE
COLLET

Born in France but based in London, Carole Collet has strong feelings about sustainability, just as she has strong views about technology, material science and design in general. Since establishing the MA Textile Futures programme at Central Saint Martins College of Art and Design in 2001, Collet has gained a reputation as one of the most maverick movers and shakers in the field today. She established the Textile Futures degree course at a time when textile innovation tended to be overshadowed by the other design disciplines, or overlooked altogether. As sustainability became a buzzword in the industry, Collet was surprised to see how cold-wash cottons and hemp-heavy weaves began to symbolize the innovations that would make textiles more environmentally friendly. At the time, Collet was busy forging alliances with biochemists, material scientists and biomimetic engineers, and she could see that science held a wide range of sustainable solutions that had the potential to revolutionize the industry.

Collet's starting point is usually the translation of an idea into materiality, a process in which the conservation of resources is paramount. She says: 'Sustainability is just a natural part of the design process, not something that you try to add to the process later on. Managing resources, minimizing waste and staying away from harmful chemicals should be second nature to textile designers. I can heighten the sustainability that's already there by designing textiles that don't drain any resources at all. Fabrics that generate the energy they need to perform, and textiles capable of replicating themselves exemplify this.'

For the Nobel Textiles initiative in 2008, Collet teamed up with John Sulston, an award-winning human genome scientist whose research into the cell death process identified the first mutation of one of the participating genes. 'My contribution was a design based on the concept of "suicide cells" that shape our body,' Collet explains. 'It made me think about labile forms that morph into new shapes as they biodegrade.'

The cell death research carried out by Sulston examines the process whereby the cells of a developing foetus die off voluntarily so that other cells can develop and function more fully. 'I was fascinated by the discovery that all organisms produce more cells than they need, and that this biological process actually shapes and sculpts forms,' Collet explains. 'I translated John's research into a biodegradable textile called "Suicidal Pouf", designed for the garden, which sheds fibres over time to reveal its final form.'

Collet is keen to dispel the idea that the future of textiles has to be based in technology alone. 'Technology holds exciting applications for the future, but so does Mother Nature,' she says. 'I love being surrounded by nature; it's a source of inspiration for me personally, but also a place to identify sources of innovation that apply to textile design in general. To me, the sun and the wind can be expressed in textile form as solar energy and movement. Look at how

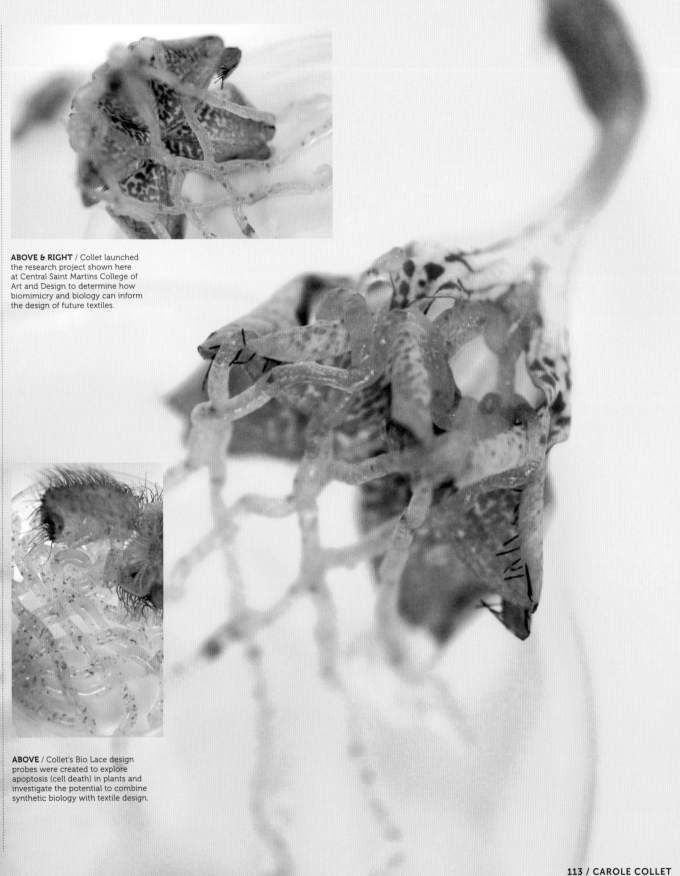

ABOVE & RIGHT / Collet launched the research project shown here at Central Saint Martins College of Art and Design to determine how biomimicry and biology can inform the design of future textiles.

ABOVE / Collet's Bio Lace design probes were created to explore apoptosis (cell death) in plants and investigate the potential to combine synthetic biology with textile design.

the sunflower can open and close, and lock onto the sun, moving its face in sync with the sun's movements in the sky. I found out from Richard Bonser, a biomimetic scientist based at Brunel University, London, that plants and flowers are able to perform movements through osmosis, the passage of water through their cells. I realized that osmosis could be mimicked by a textile as well.'

The textiles Collet designs are groundbreaking in their innovative use of resources and materials. By forming alliances with scientists and researchers, Collet is pioneering new directions for traditional textile forms. 'The more I find out about biological processes, the more I see their applications for textile designs,' Collet says. 'Many provide a model that could inspire a design for sustainable fabric in future.'

ALL IMAGES / Collet constructed a macramé pouf from abaca, jute, sisal and nylon rope. The combination of a biodegradable surface and a resilient nylon core resulted in an organic form that would change shape over time. Collet looped the jute, abaca and sisal across the poufs' surfaces, giving them shaggy exteriors; as they degrade and disappear, the textured surface beneath becomes more visible. This effect mimics the biological process of cell death. The Suicidal Textiles collection was showcased as part of the Medical Research Council's 2008 Nobel Textiles exhibition at the Institute of Contemporary Art in London.

TOP RIGHT, ABOVE & LEFT /
Pop Up Lace is the first industrially produced lace made from a paper yarn. The project was manufactured as a limited edition by Sakae for Warp Factor 2009, a Central Saint Martins College of Art & Design touring exhibition held in Tokyo, Guangzhou and London.

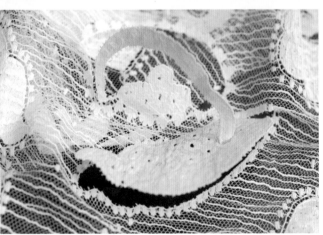

TOP LEFT / Pop Up Lace is made from paper yarn and nylon. The project was commissioned for Warp Factor 2009, a Central Saint Martins College of Art and Design touring exhibition held in Tokyo, Guangzhou and London.

Carole Collet forges alliances with biochemists, scientists and biomimetic engineers to develop sustainable solutions so advanced they may revolutionize the industry.

LEFT / The Pop Up Lace project takes a playful look at the ritualistic aspect of textiles used in a dining context.

EMILY CRANE

A designer is a very tricky thing to be these days. When conventional materials no longer appeal, some designers have to resort to creating their own. Emily Crane is just such a designer. Following her fashion studies, London-based Crane set out to pioneer a fresh direction for clothing by finding materials and processes that could take the discipline forwards. When none of the textiles and techniques she was looking for could be found, Crane began to cultivate and grow new hybrid materials of her own.

Disillusioned by mass manufacturing and the tremendous amount of waste it produces, Crane decided to take a 'zero resources' approach to making garments. 'I started envisioning a future where fashion is sustainable yet still has a quick turnover,' Crane says. An interest in food science inspired Crane to set up a materials lab in her kitchen, where she began to combine sugars, proteins and foaming agents to create wearable membranes made from basic cooking ingredients. 'I cook, blend and work with live cultures to make materials I can manipulate to create fashion fabrics, accessories and whole garments,' Crane explains. 'Some of my materials are grown rather than made, and I freeze bubbles to create a form of bio-lace that is both wearable and edible.' All of Crane's materials are made from edible ingredients. Thickening agents such as gelatines and starches, and seaweeds such as carrageenan and agar-agar are combined with natural flavourings, glycerine and

LEFT & BOTTOM LEFT / Mass-manufacturing generates huge amounts of textile waste, with as much as 15% of fabric lost at the cutting stage. Crane's approach is to use zero resources and eliminate cutting techniques that create waste.

BELOW / Made from food ingredients, the jewellery-like Bio-L007 body adornment is described as an example of 'kitchen couture'.

food colouring. The genre Crane established came to be known as 'micro-nutrient couture'. The materials developed within it offer practitioners a sustainable alternative to using conventional textiles, woven and non-woven fabrics, and trims made from fibres. 'It takes innovative fabrics to create a sustainable fashion experience in an industry that constantly presents "the new",' Crane explains. 'My work offers a fresh alternative to the compulsive shopper obsessed with fast fashion, high street consumption and garments so cheap they get thrown away after use.'

Micro-nutrient couture explores a sensory world of transient materials, which smell and taste good enough to eat. 'In developing new materials I

have laid an innovative, creative foundation for future fashion design,' Crane says. 'I want to move far away from the disastrous impact that the current fashion cycles have on the planet. Food ingredients will always be produced, so being able to find ways to make innovative fashion materials and clothing from them means that fewer resources have to be allocated towards making textiles and processing them. Micro-nutrient couture can make fashion so original that no one but the wearer can use it.'

Crane's 'Bubble Dress' is a prototype for future fashion. Anticipating a day when future governments may choose to curtail trend-based fashions, Crane reacted by creating a dress that won't end up in landfill sites. 'The Bubble Dress is an example of a garment that could be made from zero-waste materials,' Crane says. 'Survival is a key inspiration for my processes. The dress doesn't hinder the survival of other organisms by polluting the environment, but as it is made from edible materials, it could promote the wearer's ability to survive.'

Through her unique approach to developing new materials, Crane has created an innovative means of taking fashion design forwards. 'I am conscious of the environmental impact that the current fashion system has on the planet,' Crane says. 'Future fashion will not be a thing of simple beauty, but of nutrition and sustainability too.'

RIGHT / This dress was made in Crane's kitchen using only food products including beef gelatine, glycerine and food colouring.

LEFT & BELOW / The materials
Crane develops provide sustainable
alternatives to conventional textiles.
The food ingredients she uses are
grown and harvested without harming
the environment. When disposed of,
they compost easily and biodegrade
almost immediately.

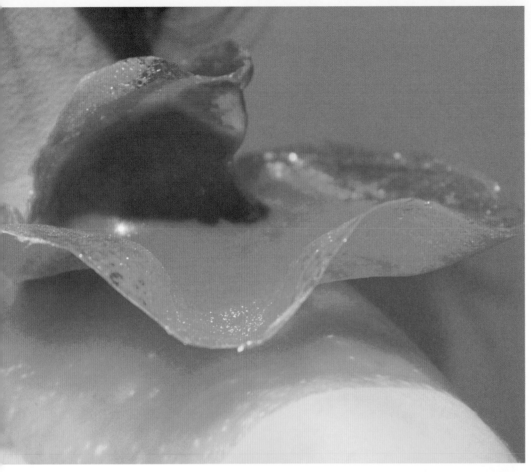

ABOVE / This skin adornment was created from Crane's Bio-L-003 Mixture. By using a range of different heat treatments and cooling processes, Crane is able to sculpt expressive shapes.

TOP RIGHT / Many of Crane's creations begin their life in a beaker being blended into wearable – and edible – designs. Here, the Bio-L-003 Mixture is shown in its liquid state.

RIGHT / By adding natural, edible dyes or food colouring, Crane can produce almost any colour and dilute it to create tones and nuances.

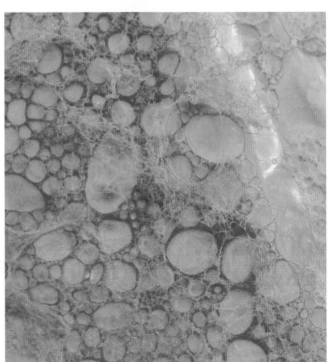

Emily Crane uses nutrients to create wearable membranes, enabling the wearer to experience a sensory world of transient materials, which smell and taste good enough to eat.

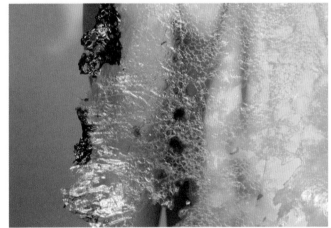

TOP & ABOVE / These two garments were made from water, gelatine and kappa carrageenan. Both are unique garments that will be worn only once and then biodegrade quickly.

RIGHT / Most of Crane's textile materials are formed in glass containers. Crane experiments with different combinations of sugars, proteins and foaming agents until she creates the consistency needed to form a wearable membrane.

BELOW / This close-up of the Bio-L-049 material shows how closely the material can simulate lace. Like non-woven techno lace, Crane's 'lace' is also made by a foam process.

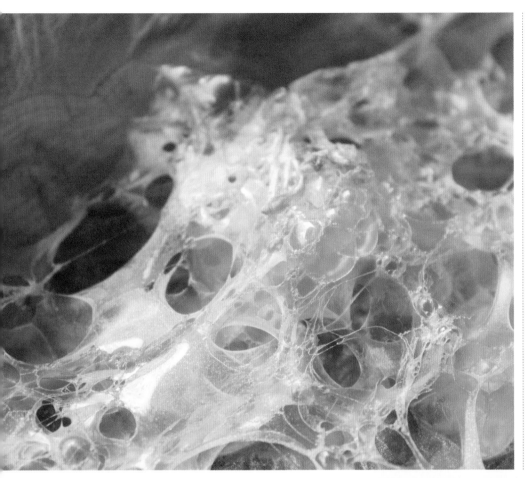

THIS PAGE / Crane experiments with structures that occur naturally when edible ingredients are cooked. Bubbles are relatively easy to 'cook up' and give Crane's materials an innovative structure that creates unique patterns.

RIGHT / Storey's Wonderland project featured 'disappearing dresses' made from water-soluble PVA (polyvinyl alcohol), a synthetic polymer, that bio-degraded when simply soaked in water. One of the dresses is shown here, immersed in a vat of water.

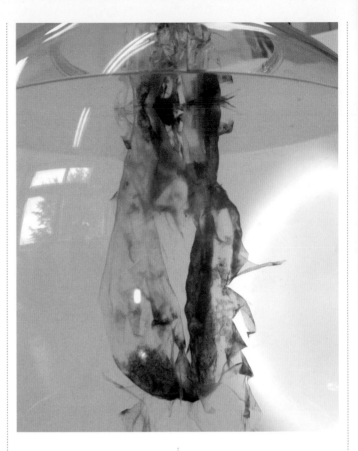

HELEN STOREY

Fashion designer Helen Storey has a vision for a new generation of intelligent materials that can sense when they are no longer needed, and automatically biodegrade into substances capable of growing new forms. Storey's collaborations with textile designer Trish Belford at the University of Ulster, and chemist Professor Tony Ryan from Sheffield University led to the development of environmentally friendly materials that have applications in fashion and textile design, as well as packaging and manufacturing.

Storey's own fashion designs have been made in a variety of fabrics, ranging from natural fibres to latex, plastics and rubber, but these days she is more likely to make her work using the PVA and photocatalytic materials she is pioneering.

New materials began to interest Storey when her work on a packaging design project seemed to reach a creative dead end. 'At the time I was reading a book about quantum mechanics to find out more about the exchanges between energy and matter,' Storey says, 'and suddenly the idea of making "intelligent" packaging that could dematerialize came to me.' Storey started with the idea of making a bottle from materials that would have an intelligent relationship with the bottle's contents and automatically disappear when it was empty. 'Think of a shampoo bottle that disappears when the last drops are squeezed out, or a "drink me – shrink me" bottle that morphs into a tiny compostable ball when all the liquid has been poured out.'

ABOVE & RIGHT / As the material begins to break down, the dresses dissolve, creating a vibrant kaleidoscope of colours in the water as they break apart. The material behaves like the individual pouches containing liquid laundry detergent, eventually disappearing altogether.

LEFT & ABOVE / Not only is Storey making fashion more eco-friendly, she's even creating garments that clean up the environment around them. Storey teamed up with scientists to develop fabric coatings that filter pollution out of the air without bringing them into contact with the wearer's skin.

OPPOSITE / Helen Storey is experimenting with methods to infuse clothing with photocatalysts during the conventional washing cycle. The result will be items of clothing that break down airborne pollutants and purify the air around them.

Storey teamed up with Ryan and the two experimented with a pre-existing PVA (polyvinyl alcohol), a water-soluble synthetic polymer that they adapted for the project. 'The PVA can be made into a substrate similar to cling film and used like fabric; it then breaks down completely when it comes into contact with water,' Storey explains. The PVA was used to create prototype 'dissolving bottles' that dissolve under hot water to form a gelatinous compost-like substance into which seeds can be planted and grown. The material could potentially revolutionize the textile industry on many levels, providing an antidote to some of the issues surrounding discarded garments and textile waste.

Trish Belford used the material Storey and Ryan developed to make dissolving textiles and created a collection of disappearing dresses from them. The dresses were exhibited on metal frames and gradually lowered into transparent vats of water. As the material began to break down, the dresses appeared to dissolve, creating a vibrant kaleidoscope of colours in the water. 'So far, the dresses made from the material are not for wear,' Storey explains. 'They are meant to spark discussions about the environmental sustainability of our current fashion system.'

Textile forms provided Storey with another means of tackling environmental pollution when she initiated a project to improve air quality. Storey extracted the technology used in catalytic converters and adapted it for fibres, then applied it to wearable garments capable of neutralizing airborne toxins. 'The two biggest sources of airborne pollutants are manufacturing and motor vehicles,' Storey explains. 'Catalytic convertor technology does prevent most of the toxins they create from reaching the air, but not all of them.' Storey's catalytic method works by harnessing the energy of photocatalysts, agents that are activated by light. 'When light shines on the photocatalysts, the electrons in the material are rearranged and subsequently they become more reactive,' Storey explains. 'These electrons are then able to react with the water in the air and split it into two radicals, which then react with the pollutants and break them down into substances that aren't harmful.'

The photocatalysts are dispersed across the garment's surface during normal laundering, where they are added to the wash with a product such as a fabric conditioner. The active agents bind to the surface of the clothing during the washing cycle and remain in place when the garment is dried. 'We know that exposure to airborne pollutants presents a risk to human health and also has a detrimental effect on ecosystems and vegetation,' Storey says. According to figures released by Kings College London in 2008, 29,000 people died from lung-related disease caused by air pollution in the UK.

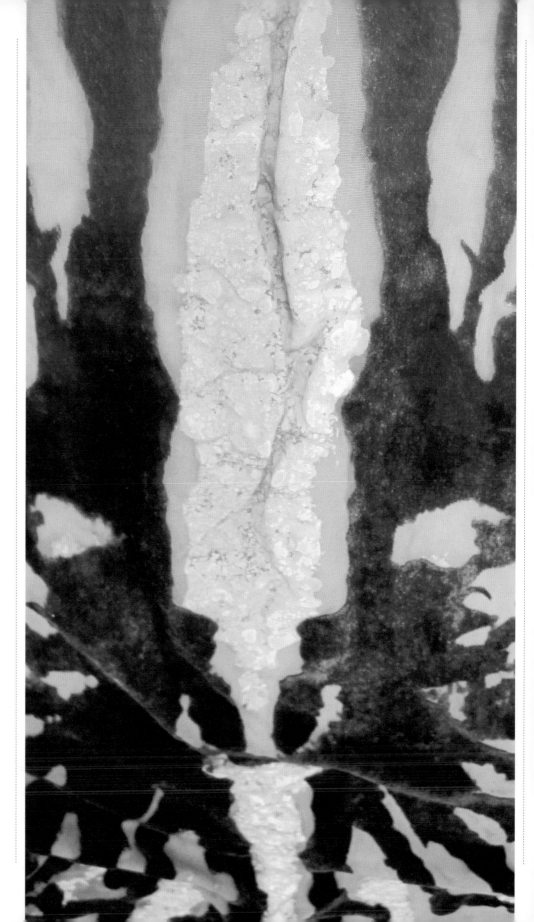

ALL IMAGES / Storey merged textile technology with science and biology to explore how clothing could be used as catalytic filters to purify air. The garments are coated with photocatalysts, networks of electrons that break down airborne pollutants into substances that aren't harmful, finding a new use for conventional catalytic convertor technology.

Helen Storey's designs are not always made to wear. The fabrics she develops are meant to spark discussions about the environmental impact of the fashion industry, and they do.

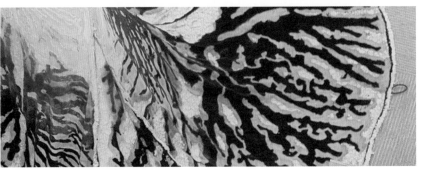

INDIA
FLINT

A new language of colour and motif is being created by natural dye expert India Flint, who experiments with the trees and plants of the Australian landscape to discover original pigments and novel dye processes. Finding ways to describe her approach is sometimes difficult, because many of her works straddle the divide between tradition and innovation, or move between serendipity and careful planning.

Flint has been interested in natural dyes since she was a child, and her fascination with the colours and patterns found in plant life has been with her ever since. 'Every Easter, the family would gather around the kitchen table to wrap hen's eggs in layers of onion skins,' Flint says. 'In between the skins, we would insert leaves, herbs such as sage, thyme, basil, mint and marjoram. The wrapped eggs were boiled, and when they cooled down enough to remove the onion skins we would find delicate leaf prints on the shells, against a background of golden brown patterns created by the onion skins.' When she grew up, Flint incorporated the technique into her textile practice, coming up with a method she calls 'ecoprint'; an ecologically sound, sustainable dye method that transfers colour to cloth by direct contact.

The ecoprint method can be employed using almost every plant, as most will yield at least one shade of colour. Determining the plant's sensitivity to heat is an important factor in extracting colour pigments, as is giving the plant enough time to secrete its colours. 'The most important thing of all is to find out as much about the plant you're working with as you can,' Flint says. 'Know its characteristics before you start harvesting its colours. Clearly, plants that are toxic or poisonous should be avoided, as should those that are rare or protected.'

Fashioning fabrics from natural forms has been a lifelong inspiration for Flint, who grew up in a home where many things were made by hand. 'At home we were surrounded by dresses, knitwear and furniture we'd made ourselves.' Flint says, 'My grandmother inspired us with stories of a princess who got lost in the forest and had to make her clothing from leaves, grass and tufts of animal fur snagged on twigs. I used to imagine her crafting a dress from leaves she pinned together with thorns and embellished with dewdrops, fireflies and luminous beetles.'

Her grandmother's wisdom was channelled by Flint a second time when she was searching for an alternative to chemical dyes. 'I was becoming disenchanted by synthetic colours and worried about their ecological impact,' Flint says. 'I remembered how my grandmother used garden plants to overdye her clothes, and began to experiment more seriously with plant dyes.' Flint found that the dyestuff values of Australian plants such as the eucalyptus had already been well documented, so she began to look around for lesser-known alternatives she could explore. 'The penny really dropped for me when I collected eggs from the hidden nest of a broody hen after three days of rain,' she said. 'I found that the eucalyptus leaves she had used to line her nest

OPPOSITE, LEFT & BOTTOM / Not only are India Flint's textiles inspired by nature, but they also seem to belong to it. As a child she was inspired by a fairytale about a lost princess who made her clothing from grass, leaves and tufts of animal fur, and today she explores the trees and plants of the Australian landscape to discover original pigments and natural dyes.

OPPOSITE, RIGHT / Eucalyptus leaves are covered with oil glands but also contain rich pigments. Flint uses heat processes and natural substances to harvest the colours within the leaves and create a lasting print on fabric.

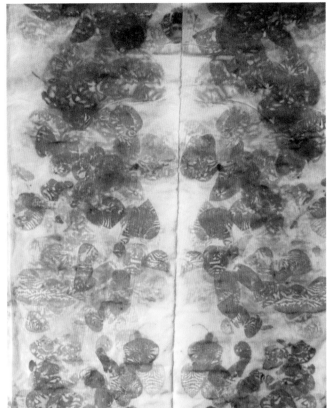

had made lasting impressions on the shells of her eggs by using nothing more than moisture and the hen's body heat.' The hen's nest sparked Flint to experiment with low-grade heat processes, which led to techniques that don't require synthetic adjuncts. 'From my research into the eucalyptus, I had thought that metallic salt mordants had to be added to make the colour fast,' Flint explains. 'Clearly, these weren't actually necessary.'

Flint's colour palette of dyes ranges from the vibrant green of fresh leaves to brilliant reds, golds and rich chocolate browns. Flint captures the soft blue-greys and dull greens of picked leaves as they appear in nature, or processes them in vessels made from metals such as copper, aluminium, zinc and iron to create further variations of colour. 'Lately I've been working with autumn leaves, discovering that even maples collected from the gutters can make beautiful prints on cloth,' Flint says. 'It's simply magic, just like in the fairytale.'

RIGHT & OPPOSITE / The garments designed for Flint's fashion label are 'ecoprinted' using her signature technique. The cloth is layered with leaves then rolled up and treated with moisture and heat to capture the leaves' impressions.

BELOW / Every textile Flint dyes is unique. Rather than develop specific formulas that can be repeated, Flint relies on her intuition and the materials she has to hand, even manipulating water quality by choosing specific vessels to affect the final outcome of the dye process.

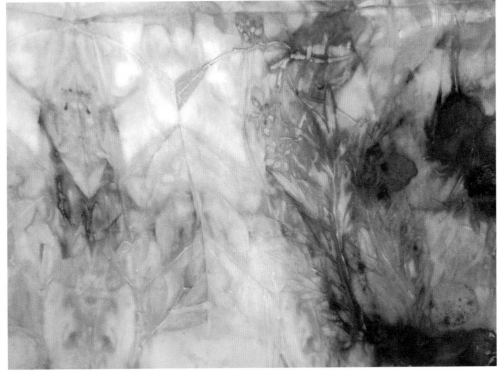

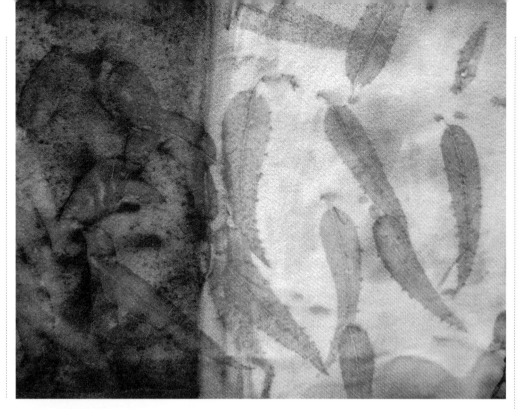

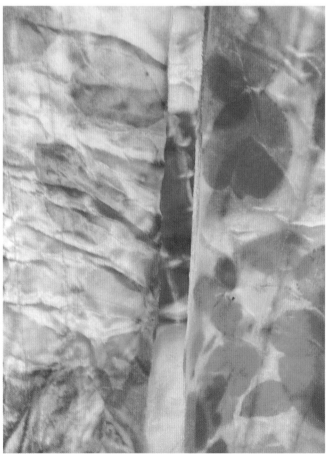

India Flint developed a dye method she calls 'ecoprint'; an ecologically sound, sustainable dye process that transfers colour to cloth by direct contact.

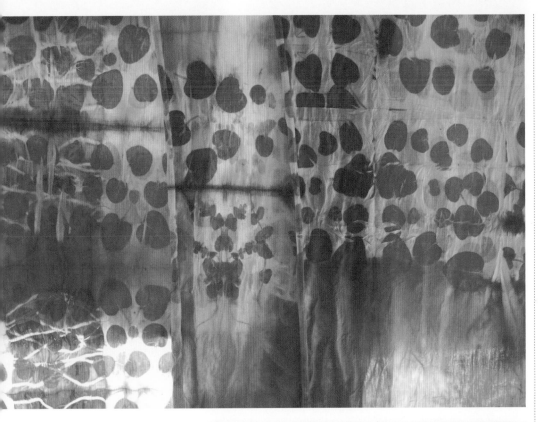

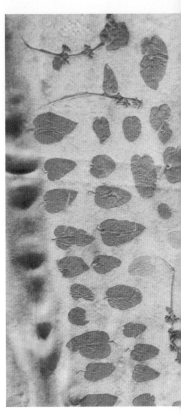

TOP LEFT/ Leaves from the *Eucalyptus Cinerea* tree are often used in Flint's dye processes. Because the leaves have different pigment properties at each stage of their growth, Flint harvests them in the juvenile leaf phase to capture the rich red tones shown here.

LEFT & OPPOSITE / Flint used high-quality merino blends, which are scoured, knitted, cut and sewn in Australia. The Milkymerino™ cloth, produced by growers in New South Wales, is ecoprinted using eucalyptus leaves. Flint describes merino wool and eucalyptus leaves as 'a match made in heaven' since the leaves' pigments fix to the fibres quickly.

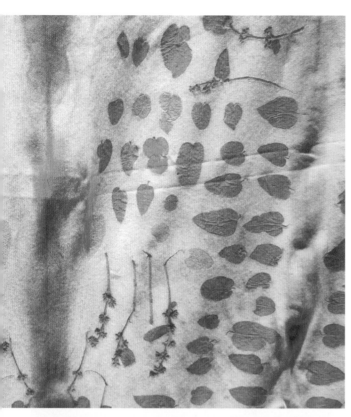

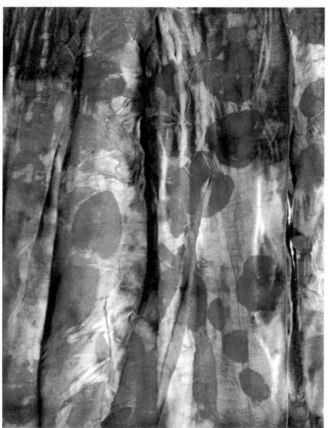

LEFT & BELOW / The *Eucalyptus Crenulata* species is found in the Acheron River valley in Victoria, Australia. The leaf outlines feature in many of Flint's dye transfers and the leaves themselves are sometimes added directly to the dye baths.

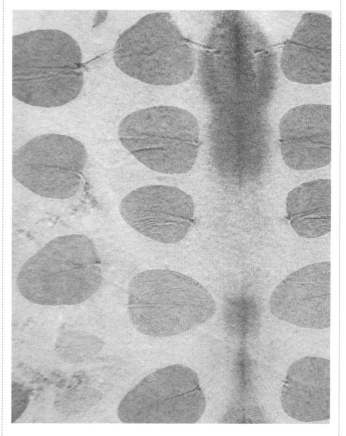

ABOVE / Lupins have orchid-like blossoms. They resemble ornamental plants but grow like wildflowers. Flint extracts dyes from the flowers and freezes them before adding them to the dye bath. The motifs shown here were made by lupin leaves.

LEFT & BOTTOM / Flint's Leaf Wrap prints were made using stalks cut from rose bushes. The bundles were wrapped in fabric and processed to extract the green pigments from the leaves. Flint sprinkled small fragments of iron among the leaves to create a chemical change that created the purple colours.

BELOW / Several different types of eucalyptus plants feature in Flint's work. Leaves, bark and flowers from *Eucalyptus Globulus, Eucalyptus Sideroxylon* and *Eucalyptus Citriodora* are used to create browns, pinks and purples, while leaves from the *Eucalyptus Cinerea* create the rich red colours shown here.

RIGHT / Samanidou combines
weaving and drawing, two
traditional creative skills that she
aligns with modern digital
design tools.

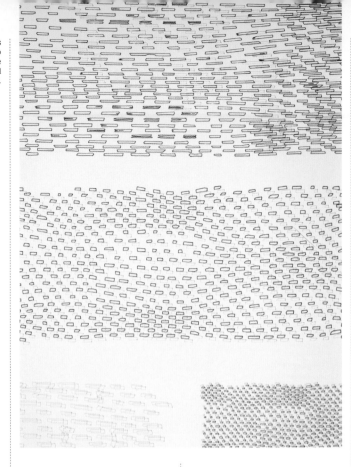

ISMINI
SAMANIDOU

When it comes to textile innovation, award-winning designer Ismini Samanidou is one of the first names that comes to mind. Known for creating new and original methods, London-based Samanidou combines traditional craft skills and organic materials with digital design tools. The new modes of design she creates are as sustainable as they are exciting. 'I am intrigued by the possibilities that result when craft and digital technologies are combined,' Samanidou says. 'They often result in works that are made without wasting resources, and are fabricated more efficiently, making them last longer. Bringing the designer-maker closer to the kinds of digital and industrial technologies that can produce artistic works creates a better outcome.'

In her own practice, Samanidou uses digital technologies to relay information about different materials to the production process, and to sync the exchanges of data between them. 'The techniques I develop wholly integrate digital technologies with designer-maker practice,' Samanidou explains. 'I mainly use a computerized Jacquard loom for weaving my designs, and even though it is an industrial machine, I use a traditional weavers' making method of changing the designs and materials intuitively as I am weaving.'

The textiles that Samanidou produces are mainly super-sized works made for exhibitions and art collectors, and they are often architectural in scale. Samanidou's extraordinary 16 x 3m (53 x 9ft) *Timeline*

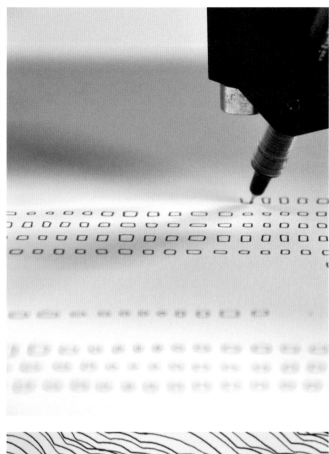

ABOVE / Together with designer Gary Allson, Samanidou explores the extent to which weaving could be combined with the milling techniques that shape wood. The process begins with digital drawings, as shown above. The machine can create single geometric shapes or overlay several, or draw contours and curves.

installation, for example, which was a site-specific piece woven at the Oriole Mill in North Carolina to be exhibited at London's Jerwood Space, is among the largest textiles ever displayed in Britain. The installation was commissioned for the Jerwood Contemporary Makers exhibition in 2009, where it spanned the full length of the gallery, dividing it into several different areas. 'The project pushed the boundaries of what could be created with a Jacquard loom,' Samanidou says. 'The textile was so big that it had architectural proportions, which was a challenge to create using a loom that normally produces runs of fashion fabrics or interior textiles.' Samanidou's perseverance paid off, resulting in a pioneering textile that portends a new relationship between textiles and architecture. 'The textile illustrated the story of the space itself, weaving a space within the space,' she says.

Although Samanidou's work breaks new ground, the time-honoured weaving techniques she uses situate her work among the most enduring craft forms. Samanidou considers weaving to be one of the most sustainable techniques used today, and points out that its longevity and potential to create works with high production values sets it apart from other methods. 'Sustainability is an important aspect of my practice in terms of creating woven work which will be valued, preserved and passed on to future generations,' Samanidou says. 'When working with students, I communicate the importance of considering the materials and processes involved in making work, and encourage students to think about how the

work will exist in the future.' In 2008, Samanidou teamed up with product designer Gary Allson to explore the extent to which weaving could be combined with the milling techniques that shape wood. Samanidou and Allson replicated woven structures in wood, creating a series of milled timber pieces that replicate woven fabrics such as twill, which they titled 'Woven Wood'. 'We used digital design tools to translate my 2-D drawings into 3D data, which was then downloaded electronically by a 3D milling machine to produce wood panels,' Samanidou says. The designs that resulted are used as architectural panels for both interior and exterior applications.

Samanidou says she will continue to fuse hand-craftsmanship with digital methods in future, and is planning to use hand looms alongside milling machines, and digital design tools in conjunction with watercolour brushes and ink pens. 'In my own work and in my collaborative projects, I am driven by an investigation into how weaving can exist within architectural space,' Samanidou says. 'I believe this creates a new value for weaving, highlighting its beauty, longevity and sustainability, while creating works that can be enjoyed by generations to come.'

ALL IMAGES / Samanidou
and Allson's work includes textiles,
wood and computer numerically
controlled drawings on paper, shown
here, which are studies for the works
Samanidou and Allson produce. A
narrative behind the work references
ephemera and the impermanence of
the man made. The marks on paper
shown here recreate the texture and
patina of cloth and are sometimes
displayed along with the textiles or
wooden pieces they relate to.

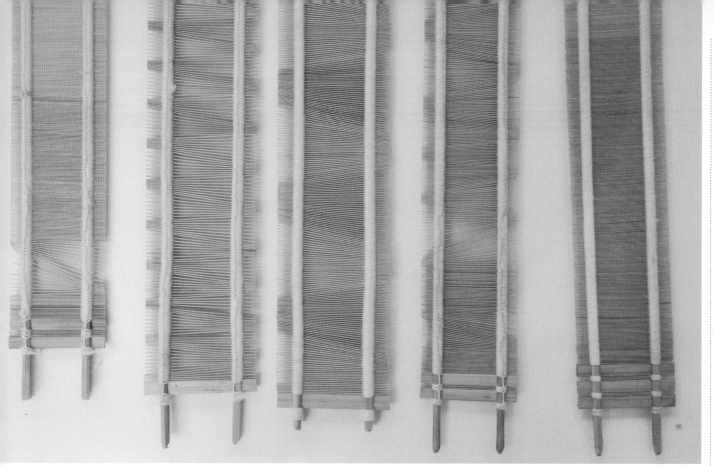

ABOVE & RIGHT / Samanidou brought these reeds back from Bangladesh, where she exchanged skills with local craftspeople while visiting. The reeds and textiles made with them were later exhibited in England to show how the unique combination of crafts, designs, textiles and opportunities in Bangladesh can inspire sustainable practices among British designers and makers.

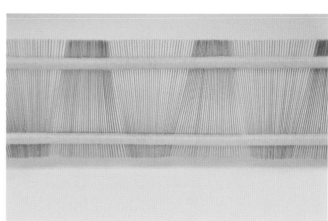

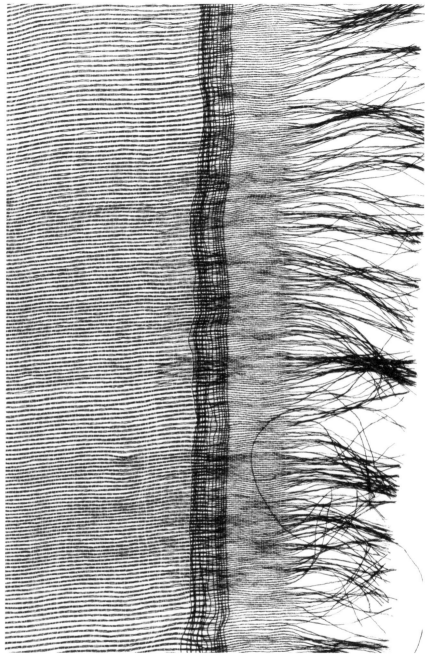

Samanidou combines traditional craft skills and natural materials with digital design tools to create new modes of design that are as sustainable as they are exciting.

TOP LEFT & ABOVE / These textiles were hand-woven using the bamboo reeds used by the local weavers of Tangail, who are well known for their Jacquard fabrics. Samanidou introduced the technique to her students in England, reviving interest in handmade fabrics.

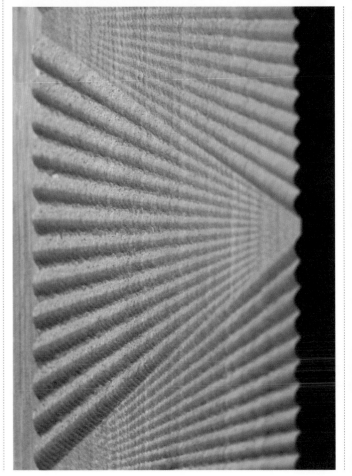

THIS PAGE / In collaboration with designer Gary Allson, Samanidou used digital making methods to translate traditional weave structures into timber surfaces using CNC milled processes. Inspired by weaves such as twill, herringbone and hopsack, Samanidou and Allson combined wood and textiles to create new surfaces. The designs that resulted, shown here, can be produced on doors, tables, screens or window panels to give them a unique look and an innovative texture.

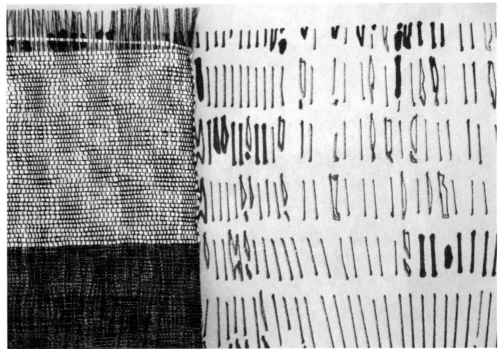

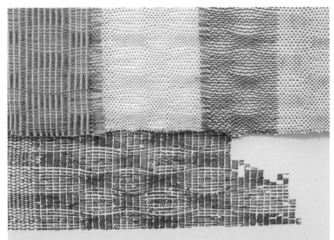

ABOVE & LEFT / Samanidou integrates digital technologies with designer-maker practice. Her hand drawings are translated into textiles on industrial looms. Many of her designs are based on photography that she translates into textures and motifs.

KELSEY ASHE

The hand-printed fashion fabrics designed by Kelsey Ashe are sumptuous textiles in all their splendour, adorned with motifs that comment on the relationships between culture, humanity and the environment. 'Ashe fabrics worship nature,' says the designer with a smile, underlining her commitment to sustainable design. 'Wherever possible, I try to source fabrics that are organically grown; or that are produced using sustainable methods. The hand-printing processes I use do not include any chlorine or formaldehyde, and dyes with toxic metals are totally banned.'

From her studio in Fremantle, just south of Perth in Western Australia, Ashe seeks fibres and fabrics from stocks that are certified 'organic'. She also enquires about the conditions in the country of origin, and refuses to buy any textiles from areas where child labour may be used. 'I am mindful of claiming to be "eco-friendly" in an industry which is renowned for waste product,' Ashe says. 'However, what I can do is make a personal contribution through choosing environmentally friendly fabrics where possible, avoiding toxic processes and recycling printed off-cuts to minimize waste. This mindful approach guides me to make small, but hopefully significant, changes.' In recent years, Ashe has seen the demand for eco-friendly fabrics rise dramatically, and noticed that consumers are increasingly concerned about fabric's origin and life cycle. 'Today, terms such as "hand-printed" and "eco-friendly" are synonymous with a set of values, which include authenticity, artistry and sustainability,' she says. 'Fabrics made from organic fibres and printed by hand have a powerful appeal to modern urban individuals. Such consumers seem to want to wear fabrics which are signifiers of their conscience, and they help the wearer create their own environmentally aware identity.'

Ashe's ideology motivates her to take her commitment to sustainability to deeper levels, even leading her to make prints that address environmental themes. Issues such as river pollution, urban litter, environmental disasters and the destruction wrought by plagues of introduced species question humankind's respect for the environment. 'The narratives are too subtle to be obvious at first glance,' Ashe says. 'I start by using the overall beauty of the print as a seductive device which will draw the viewer in. A closer look at the decorative detailing reveals hidden motifs, showing litter, polluted water, deforestation and landfill scars, acting as gentle prompts to cause consumers to contemplate how we treat the environment.'

The striking beauty of Ashe's designs, which often draw on the rich textile traditions of Asia, have attracted interest from Australia's top fashion labels, who have commissioned her to create prints for their collections. Several of them have become sell-out fashion designs, many others have adorned garments worn by celebrities and socialites. Ashe decided to launch her own fashion and homeware label 'Ashe' in 2002, creating new prints and motifs for each collection. 'I never intended to be

a fashion designer,' Ashe says. 'I studied textiles as an art practice and not as part of a fashion course. My conceptual approach to design prompts me to dig under the surface of an idea and address issues I'm passionate about.'

With a few media-acclaimed collections and a reputation for making elegant, distinctive and exotic designs, Ashe's fashion label has become a great showcase for her printed motifs. 'My fashion work evolved out of my textile practice,' Ashe says, 'and the garments are made with the same commitment to sustainability. No garment is intended to be a seasonal trend. Each is designed to be long-lasting, and some items, like my hand-printed silk gowns, have become collector pieces.' Ashe actively promotes a move away from the culture of 'throwaway chic' by crafting small runs of garments intended to be timeless in appeal and made from precious fabrics that are durable and long-lasting. 'My garments have always carried the slogan "to collect and cherish",' Ashe says. 'I often tell my customers that when they buy an Ashe dress they can look forward to handing it down to their daughter, and will perhaps even get to see it worn by their granddaughters.'

Kelsey Ashe takes sustainability to deeper levels, designing prints that address issues such as river pollution and the destruction wrought by plagues of introduced insects.

OPPOSITE PAGE / Ashe's work is rooted in Australian sensibilities but includes inspirations from the Far East and Europe. This motif combines the stark simplicity of English woodcuts with motifs that mimic eighteenth-century chinoiserie.

BELOW / When Ashe applies her textile expertise to fashion design, she has only one goal in mind: 'To make each garment as individual as the wearer'. As a result, Ashe's fashion collections feature limited-edition and one-of-a-kind garments hand-printed with her motifs.

RIGHT / Ashe had the opportunity to exchange skills with a rural textile workforce in Pakistan. There, skilled embroiderers translated her hand-drawn illustrations into beautiful textile motifs. The detail shown here is the head of a phoenix bird, drawn by Ashe.

TOP LEFT / Ashe' print catalogue consists of hundreds of patterns, some of which have been licensed to leading fashion labels. Ashe draws each by hand, as this detail of a dragonfly reveals, then uses computer applications to reconfigure them for printing on fabric.

ABOVE & TOP RIGHT / The Athena Gown is crafted in 100% silk, chosen because of its ability to drape over the body. Like the knee-length scarlet silk sash dress shown top right, Ashe's motifs adorn the surface, making her signature style immediately recognizable.

THIS PAGE / It's rare to find a single designer who demonstrates such a broad range of styles and techniques. Ashe's work is wide-ranging in scope, and she is always focussed on sustainability in her choice of materials and manufacturing processes. The motifs shown here reveal the breadth of Ashe's work: the natural, the exotic and the traditional.

LEFT / Screen-printed onto a white silk garment, the Day Waratah motif lends a surprisingly neo-Gothic element to a classic design.

RIGHT / Ashe's Day Waratah motif was inspired by the flowering plant native to the south-eastern parts of Australia. Her drawing depicts the dense flower heads and oblong leaves that characterize the plant.

ABOVE / Many of Ashe's motifs are motivated by her commitment to take sustainability to a deeper level. The motifs shown here address environmental issues such as river pollution and advocate an awareness of the plight of species on the brink of extinction.

RIGHT / Ashe's prints are used to decorate a variety of accessories, including notebooks. Her environmental motifs are intended to prompt consumers to contemplate how they treat the environment.

LAURA MARSDEN

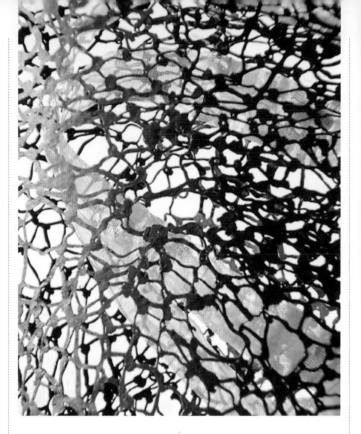

ABOVE / This detail of Marsden's signature lace textile reveals its complex structure, which is much stiffer than real lace. It can be sculpted into a variety of textures and shapes that can be worn on the body or used in interior design.

OPPOSITE / Marsden's lace wedding dress was made entirely by hand especially for the Love Lace exhibition at the Powerhouse Museum in Sydney, Australia. The dress was one of Marsden's first full-length pieces. When light falls across the surface of the dress it creates shadows that give the illusion of multiple layers.

The concept of 'life cycle textiles' is inspiring a new paradigm of manufacturing processes. Among them, 'upcycling', a process whose name was coined by William McDonough and Michael Braungart in their book, *Cradle to Cradle*, advocates refurbishing waste items to reintroduce them to the top of the consumer goods chain. British textile designer Laura Marsden is an expert in this emerging field, who pioneers new methods of transforming accumulated waste into fashion items and interior accessories.

Marsden created a method of converting waste plastic bags into base materials that can be sewn and stitched like fabric. By combining hand-stitching techniques and needle-lace making with other processes, Marsden transformed the properties and appearance of the plastic bags. 'I named the technique "Eternal Lace",' Marsden explains. 'The textile that resulted is lacy in appearance but is much stiffer than real lace. It can be sculpted in a wide range of shapes and has many potential uses in fashion and interior design.'

Eternal Lace is crafted entirely by hand, making each piece a one-off. Marsden describes the fashion items she makes as 'neck pieces' that can be worn like jewellery, or attached to garment like a collar. A collection of one-off fashion pieces is also in the works. A dress made from Eternal Lace showed that handmade fashion could rival couture without being crafted from high-quality fabrics or created using complex tailoring techniques. 'My work preserves traditional hand-stitching methods while making them relevant to today's society,' Marsden says. Although her work finds contemporary expression for traditional craftsmanship, paradoxically, historical costume, particularly Elizabethan ruffs and cuffs, is the inspiration behind it.

The interior accessories Marsden designs appear to be completely rooted in the present day. Using Eternal Lace, Marsden crafts cushion covers, wall hangings, interior screens and an assortment of ornaments. Integrating Eternal Lace into cushion covers resurfaces them with rich textures that are as tactile as they are beautiful. 'The interior pieces are inspired by organic forms and conceived as decorative, sculptural objects,' Marsden explains. 'They lend unusual, eye-catching textures to the interior, and cast ethereal shadows on the surfaces around them. The wall hangings are made in several sizes, ranging from 30cm (12in) to 60cm (24in) in diameter. I call them "Blooms" because they appear to have opened and expanded, just like blossoming flowers.' Marsden's work reveals that virtually all discarded fabrics have the potential to acquire fresh life in new form, making the concept of textile waste redundant. As she continues to develop new processes, Marsden shows how studio-based practices and traditional craftsmanship can be combined to reprocess waste. 'My practice is devoted to transforming the recycling of textiles in new, innovative ways,' Marsden says. 'I enjoy manipulating fabrics and challenging existing techniques. I'm committed to ensuring that the results challenge preconceptions about the desirability of recycled products.'

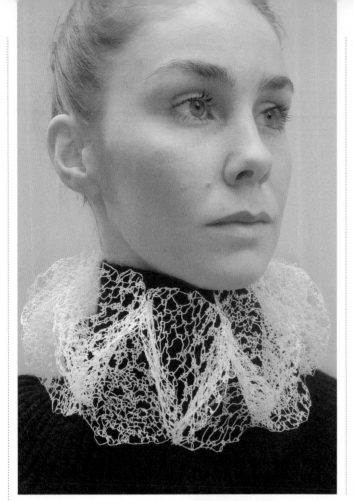

THIS PAGE / Marsden's lace is made from waste plastic, giving material destined for landfills new life as interior textiles, fashion accessories and wall adornments. Marsden's grey ruff (above right) is a contemporary accessory inspired by a historic shape; it is one of two pieces purchased by the Victoria & Albert Museum in London for their permanent Contemporary Collection, and is made out of plastic bags from their Art Deco exhibition. Marsden's eternal lace cushions (right) bring elements of sustainable style to the home.

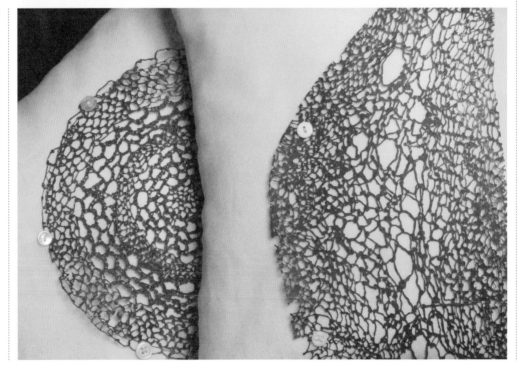

RIGHT / The unique structural characteristics of Marsden's lace enable it to hold its shape in ways that organic textiles seldom do. The lace headdress, shown here, moulds itself to the head and veils the face like traditional lace netting would.

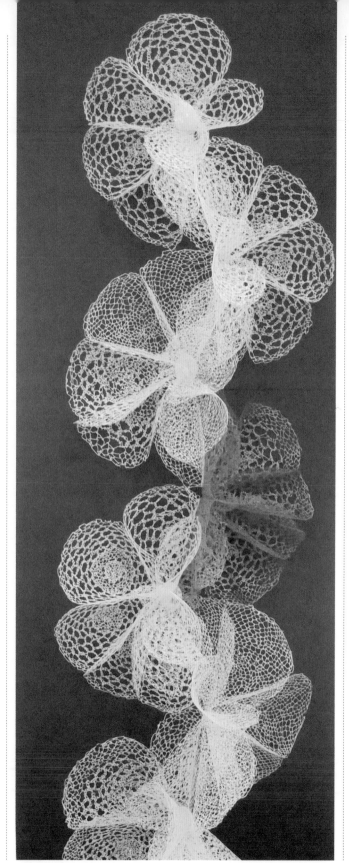

ALL IMAGES / The wall adornments Marsden designs and makes are inspired by organic forms. They are decorative, but also sculptural, and cast distinctive shadows on the surfaces around them. They can be grouped together to form a serpentine chain, or mounted on the wall individually.

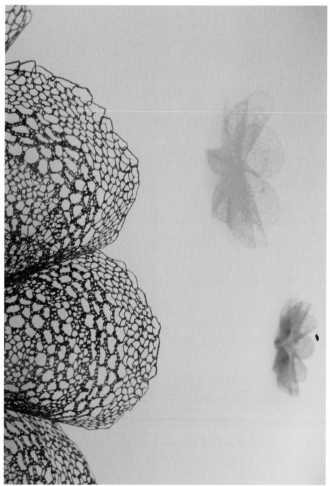

Laura Marsden shows how easily discarded fabrics and pieces of plastic can acquire fresh life in new form, making the concept of textile waste completely redundant.

MARGOT SELBY

Craft traditions meet cutting-edge contemporary textiles in the work of London-based designer Margo Selby, who creates luxury fabrics for everyday use. In the five short years that her studio has been established, she has launched lines of interior textiles, established a consultancy practice and initiated various collaborative projects with fashion designers, architects and artists. She has developed limited-edition products with national galleries and museums, and has won numerous craft and design awards.

Selby is a specialist in woven textiles who trained at Chelsea College of Art and Design before pursuing a postgraduate degree at the Royal College of Art. Weaving is at the core of Selby's practice, and central to her vision of the future of textiles. Selby's fabrics are acclaimed for their luxurious feel and bold colourways. Most originate on the 24-shaft dobby loom in Selby's workroom, where she and her staff experiment with new weave structures and fibre combinations. 'I started my career hand-weaving organic yarns on a loom in my bedroom,' she says. 'The hand-woven step of the textile process is central to everything I design, and it is from there that I create fabrics for production at the mills.'

When Selby finished her studies, she spent the next 18 months as a fellow at the Ann Sutton Foundation, a research centre for woven textiles. During her time with the foundation, the projects she developed for industry were tantamount to pursuing her own practice. While there, Selby found ways to adapt her hand-woven designs for industrial looms, creating the unique, three-dimensional fabrics that were to become the trademark of her brand. 'These days there is a lot of emphasis on techno textiles,' she says, 'which are taking the industry forward. I really like all the textile innovations emerging now, yet I think there is still a lot to be learned from hand-woven designs.'

Selby never set out to be a sustainable designer, as such, but the traditional weaving methods she uses are the basis for most sustainable textiles. 'There is a lot to be said for natural dyes and traditional methods of spinning and threading silk fibres,' she says. 'My hand-woven scarves are made on the loom and are so popular that they sell out very quickly. I would love to spend my life working solely on a traditional handloom, but that's not a viable option for me right now. I have had to diversify my business to make my brand more commercial and affordable. Short runs are made on hand looms in my studio, while large production runs are sent to English mills to be woven to my specifications.' Once the fabrics are finished, they are dispatched to the studio where a team of specialists transforms them into a range of products. Cushions, curtains, wall panels and lampshades can be made in the studio, while Selby's rugs, travel accessories and wallpaper are made off-site.

With so much production occurring in-house, a number of off-cuts, lengths of selvedge and textile scraps are left behind after each production run. 'There is never any waste here,' Selby says. 'Anything left over from

manufacturing one product becomes material for another. The studio organizes sewing courses in the evenings and at weekends and the participants use the scraps to make things like patchwork cushions, travel bags and purses.'

Since launching her business, Margo has become recognized as a pioneer within contemporary textiles. 'Sustainability was part of my business plan when I started out,' Selby says, 'and making my production as eco-friendly as possible seems to pay off.' Selby's trademark textiles and products are sold in many shops and galleries around the world, and are fast becoming coveted contemporary classics.

RIGHT / Selby's Caroline fabric was inspired by cut gemstones and jewels. The fabric was initially designed for a jewellery boutique and is now part of Selby's main collection.

BELOW / Most of Selby's production is done in her studio in London. Here, cushions are being made from her Fiesta fabric.

OPPOSITE, TOP / The tensile properties of a wide variety of yarns are explored to create innovative surface textures. This image was taken during one of the weaving workshops Selby holds to pass traditional skills on to younger designers.

OPPOSITE, BOTTOM / This sofa was designed in collaboration with London-based furniture designer Richard Ward and manufactured by his brand, Wawa. The sofa is upholstered in Selby's Charleston fabric, inspired by the colour palette used by the Bloomsbury Group.

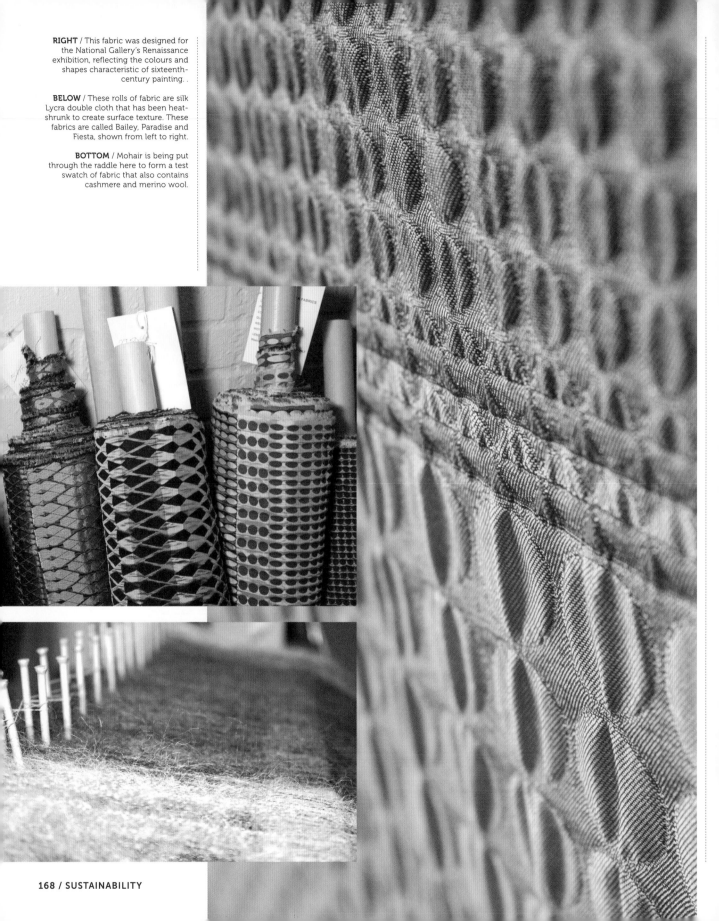

RIGHT / This fabric was designed for the National Gallery's Renaissance exhibition, reflecting the colours and shapes characteristic of sixteenth-century painting. .

BELOW / These rolls of fabric are silk Lycra double cloth that has been heat-shrunk to create surface texture. These fabrics are called Bailey, Paradise and Fiesta, shown from left to right.

BOTTOM / Mohair is being put through the raddle here to form a test swatch of fabric that also contains cashmere and merino wool.

Margo Selby operates according to a zero waste methodology. Anything left over from manufacturing one product becomes material for another.

RIGHT / The scarf shown here was hand made from mohair, cashmere and lambswool, and given a felted finish. It was commissioned by the BBC for a well-known presenter, to keep him warm in winter when filming outdoors.

BELOW / Cross sticks separate each yarn individually to prevent them from getting tangled on the loom. A traditional hand loom is shown here, but even the most technically advanced looms are threaded by hand.

BOTTOM / A boat shuttle being pulled through the warp in reverse twill to create a diamond pattern. Selby's fabric collection includes innovative fabrics as well as classic patterns like this one.

RIGHT / This sofa is upholstered in Rozelle fabric, a smooth silk blend that can withstand 30,000 rubs when tested for durability. Like the sofa shown on page 167, this one was also designed in collaboration with Richard Ward and manufactured by Wawa.

RIGHT / Mann's woven textile artworks are hand-woven on a loom, and then mounted on stretcher strips as a conventional canvas would be. This close-up shows how a variety of coloured yarns are interwoven to create subtle shifts in tone and hue.

PTOLEMY MANN

Award-winning artist and designer Ptolemy Mann takes weaving to a higher level. An expert at creating a broad spectrum of vibrant colours in a single design, she is known for her painterly approach. While still a student, Mann joined wooden stretcher strips together to create a frame, then mounted her woven textiles across them as if she was stretching a canvas. Mann's bold approach to displaying her work divided the textile establishment. Some accused her of being iconoclastic, while others hailed her methods as directional.

Since then, Mann has emerged as one of the most visionary textile designers in Britain today. Her acute awareness of colour and ability to create original colour palettes has resulted in collaborative projects with architects and fashion designers. Leading textile manufacturers, such as Christopher Farr, have commissioned Mann to design collections for them, and museums, galleries and craft centres have exhibited her work. From her studio in East Sussex, Mann carries out her own research on colour theory, the impact of pattern repeats and their effects on human behaviour. 'Obviously I'm not a scientist or a psychologist,' she says, 'but many years of working as an artist

ABOVE / The vivid surfaces of Mann's artworks may appear to clash bold colours, but Mann's practice is actually about creating transition points where two or more colours merge together.

submerged in a practical dialogue around colour has taught me to use an instinctive and sensitive approach. Observing reactions to my artwork informs how I use colour in my architectural projects. For example, I've noticed that people like the transition point created when two or more colours merge together. It stimulates the eye and engages the viewer, whether used in a small-scale textile design or a monumental architectural facade.'

Just as Mann has strong views on colour, she also makes keen observations about sustainability within textile design. 'Weaving is a sustainable practice in itself,' she says. 'It has a long history behind it, and it combines yarns and fibres in an efficient way that makes them durable and strong. I have had long discussions with various eco experts about sustainable yarns. To be truly environmentally friendly, they have to be dyed with natural pigments. Ironically, most natural dyes require a huge quantity of the ingredients to make them. For example, massive barrels of onion skins are needed to make just a small amount of orange dye, so I've been asking myself how efficient natural dyes actually are?'

For many textile designers, sustainability is a double-edged sword. As practitioners become more conscientious about the materials and processes they use, many struggle to find environmentally friendly fibres that correspond to the season's colour trends, or yield the desired finish and tactility. 'That's why I was very inspired by the lengths that Eloise Grey goes to in order to find

organic fabrics,' Mann says. 'Her ethos is "clothes to keep" and she makes dresses that last a lifetime.' Mann and Grey famously teamed up to create a series of dresses crafted in organic silk for Grey's Spring/Summer 2012 collection. The dresses were cut in Grey's signature classic style and embellished with prints designed by Mann. 'Eloise only uses sustainable fabrics and she spent a long time sourcing the organic silk for our collaboration,' Mann says. 'In the end she found it in Switzerland. We deliberately chose digital printing methods to transfer my patterns onto the silk. Digital printing is actually quite environmentally friendly because it uses just enough ink for each print. There is very little wastage and no water pollution at all.'

Mann's emphasis on quality, local partnerships and artisan-scale production runs is building a business model for small-scale textile practitioners that works. 'As a weaver, a low-impact and resourceful approach works best for me,' she says. 'Collaborative projects and the combination of traditional craft and contemporary methods can bring out the best of both worlds. Lessons learned in one discipline can inform another and create new models of sustainable design.'

RIGHT & BELOW / A collaborative venture with Ercol resulted in a collection of accessories and upholstered items.

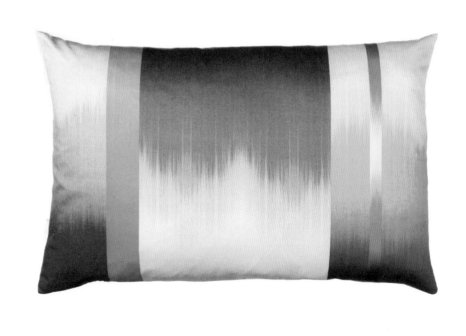

ABOVE / Vivid colour is a signature of Mann's work, making pigments and dyes a central part of her practice. Mann is selective about the synthetic dyes she uses, in some cases finding ones that have less environmental impact than natural dyes.

RIGHT & OPPOSITE PAGE, TOP / Mann describes her digitally printed fabrics as 'linear and geometric but also vibrant, exotic and painterly'. These motifs are based on bold Ikat patterns and designed to have large-scale repeats.

Mann's 'low-impact and resourceful' business model encourages local partnerships, hand-craftsmanship and materials sourced from local distributors.

ABOVE / The 'low-impact and resourceful' business model Mann follows means that wherever possible, she sources yarns, dyes and other materials from local distributors.

ABOVE LEFT & BOTTOM RIGHT /
Mann took her textile artwork in a new
direction when she moved away from
strict rectilinear shapes (such as these
wall-mounted pieces shown right) and
included round shapes (shown above).
The fabrics are woven so that they
can be evenly and uniformly mounted
over wooden stretcher shapes,
irrespective of their shape.

LEFT AND OPPOSITE PAGE /
Fashion designer Eloise Grey invited
Mann to create motifs for the organic
silk garments included in her Spring/
Summer 2012 collection. Mann used
digital printing methods to transfer
the patterns onto the silk, as the
process creates very little waste or
water pollution.

REIKO
SUDO

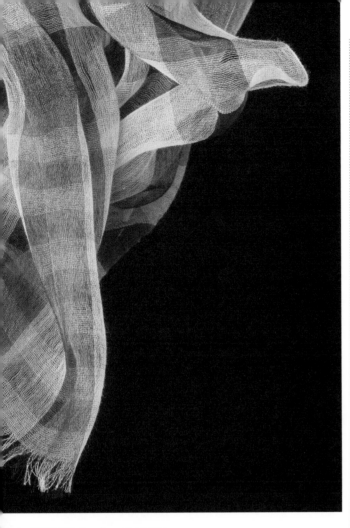

Sustainability is a core practice for today's textile designers, and some are beginning to invent new types of eco-friendly fibres and pioneer new kinds of fabrics. One of the leaders in this area is Japanese designer Reiko Sudo, who has consistently created new blends of fibres, found novel ways to produce fabrics and come up with fresh methods of recycling textile waste. From her studio in Tokyo, where her 'Nuno' brand is based, Sudo creates strikingly contemporary designs. Some are made using modern manufacturing methods; others are produced on traditional hand looms. Whether choosing organic fibres or exploring new synthetics, Sudo's approach to the application of materials and marriage of traditional craft with contemporary design is unique.

When told that her work was a model of sustainability, Sudo seemed surprised. 'Fibres are a precious resource to textile designers,' she says. 'Doesn't every designer do as much as they can to minimize waste?' However, few go to the lengths that Sudo does. Experimenting with amino acids and enzymes, and developing environmentally friendly oxidation methods, Sudo creates new ways in which fabrics can be produced, used and recycled. 'How fibres are derived is as important as their look and feel,' she says. 'I'm drawn to both fibre technology and traditional craft methods. I like to combine them and see what happens. I feel that my research provides my clients with unique fabrics that they won't find anywhere else. Knowing that they were developed in a way that doesn't harm the environment is important to them, and to me, too.'

Pointing to a handbag made by a European designer, Sudo explains why she decided to stop selling them in her Tokyo boutique. 'The designer made them from recycled waste, so no new material had to be created to make them,' she says. 'Unfortunately, they don't wear well, because the materials used to make them fall apart. The model of sustainability I follow makes things that last. The customers in my shop don't usually buy lots of textiles at once. Sometimes they choose one or two items that they say they will cherish for a lifetime, or buy a single scarf and say it's the only one they will buy this winter.' Although most of Sudo's textiles are readymade, her customers seem to approach buying her designs with the same reverence as couture clients ordering garments.

In 2001, Sudo launched a collection that explored biodegradable corn fibre and other eco-synthetics, which came to be known as the 'Eco Collection' due to the obvious use of sustainable materials. 'It felt timely to launch a sustainable collection, because there was so much interest in the subject,' Sudo says. 'But previous collections had included Bashofu, a textile from Okinawa, which is woven from banana fibre.'

Sudo created a new variety of silk enriched by a sericin amino acid produced naturally by the silkworm itself. The fabric is woven from yarns spun from kibiso, bits of fibrous outer casing on the silkworms' cocoons that workers remove to harvest the pure silk fibres inside. The cocoons' casings are formed by fibres made from the amino acids that protect the silkworm. When worn on the skin, the amino acids in the fabric help prevent oxidation, conserve moisture and even filter out UV rays. 'Creating the textile was a team effort,' Sudo says. 'I employed retired women who had been employed by the silk mill and still wanted to work today. They became actively involved in making the most of the waste silk. The silk that resulted was sustainable, and not just because it is derived from waste fibres. Producing it created a new product at the mill, which boosted the local economy and found work for women who probably would not have been able to find employment elsewhere.'

Another initiative to conserve resources resulted in a series of textiles Sudo impregnated with phosphorescent pigments. Phosphorescent materials can absorb sunlight, store it and then release it when light levels are low. In textiles, the effect is similar to glow-in-the-dark surfaces. 'I started with saran fibres, which are flame-resistant and highly water-absorbent, used mostly for sports applications,' Sudo says. 'When I impregnated the fibre with phosphorescent pigments and made it into fabric the textile gave off soft waves of light. I named the fabric 'Baby Hair' due to its delicate fibres and soft sheen.'

Sudo is leading a whole new breed of textile designers who are researching and innovating as much as they are dreaming and creating. Sudo's low-key approach to the high-profile area of sustainability is inspiring to other designers, and her

applications of both tradition and technology are paving the way for new models of sustainability.

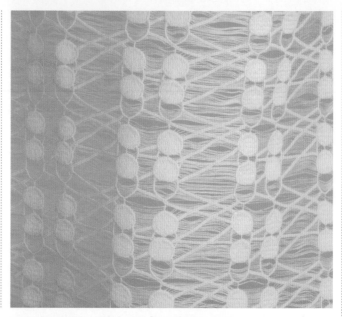

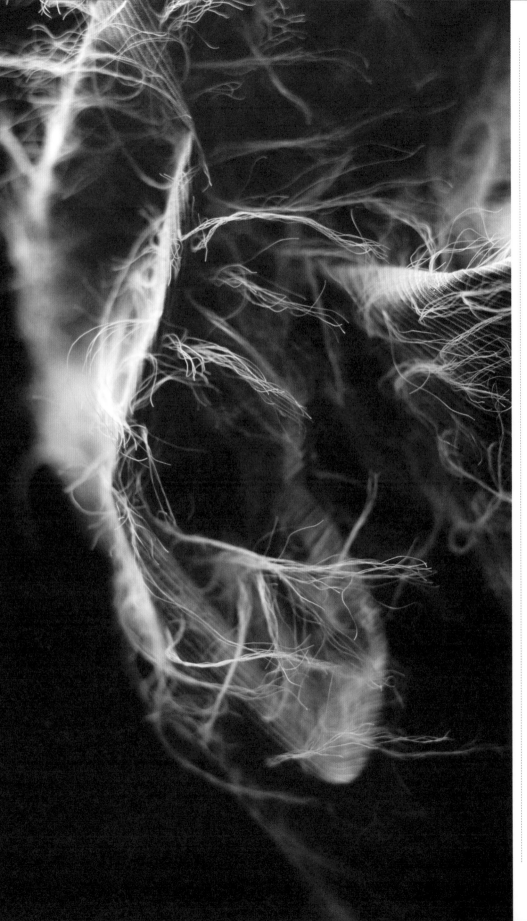

LEFT / Sudo impregnated fibres with phosphorescent materials to give a soft, glowing sheen. The phosphorescent pigments absorb sunlight, then release it when light levels are low. Sudo named the fabric Baby Hair due to its delicate fibres.

OPPOSITE, TOP / This textile, with its criss-crossing threads and series of circles, has an innovative texture. The fabric is semi-transparent, providing an ideal interior fabric for screens and window treatments.

OPPOSITE, BOTTOM / The Kasane fabric is 100% silk, designed collaboratively by Sudo and Tomoko Iida. The textile was created from fabric scraps cut to size then basted onto the silk by hand. The fabric scraps were sewn on using a conventional embroidery machine.

RIGHT / Nuno's Crisscross fabric is made from cotton and silk. The fabric is named for its two-sided double-weave that combines yarns in criss-crossing bands. The black-and-white surface that results is eye-catching and dramatic.

BELOW LEFT / The textile shown here is one of Nuno's patchwork series. The textile was created by stitching remnants of various Nuno fabrics that would otherwise have been discarded onto silk by hand.

BELOW RIGHT / Sudo is inspired by origami, the Japanese art of folding paper to create three-dimensional textures and shapes. Sudo's pleated fabric is heat-treated to make the folds permanent, creating a rich texture in the cloth.

ABOVE / Like the Baby Hair fabric shown on page 183, this fabric is woven from saran fibres which Sudo impregnated with phosphorescent pigments. The textile's soft sheen is created by the light it gives off.

RIGHT / These slippers were made from discarded fabric salvaged from a silk mill. They include fibres from the silkworm's cocoon, which is normally thrown away after the silkworm has abandoned it.

LEFT / Designed by Kazuhiro Ueno for Nuno, this Stalagmite fabric is made using a 'steering-wheel' embroidery machine, and is based on calcified rock formations.

OPPOSITE, TOP / The Tanabata design is made from 100% polyester which has been cut to create a sense of transparency.

OPPOSITE, BOTTOM / Sudo's collections often contain a considered balance of cutting-edge textile designs and contemporary classics. Every textile she designs is fully sustainable, such as the striped textile shown here.

OPPOSITE, FAR RIGHT / Nuno's Swinging Squares fabric is made from 100% cotton. The squares are embroidered to create texture and movement on the fabric's surface.

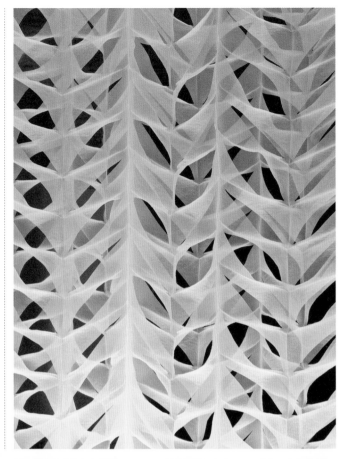

Reiko Sudo experiments with amino acids, enzymes and industrial waste materials to create environmentally friendly methods of producing, using and recycling textiles.

SHEREE DORNAN

Vintage fabrics, textile fragments, nostalgic prints and soft silks come together in Sheree Dornan's designs, creating imaginary tableaux that evoke romantic eras. Dornan's textiles evoke real worlds, too, bridging East and West, and history with the present day.

Approaching textile design from an arts background, Dornan takes a painterly approach to pattern design, and combines reclaimed fabrics with new ones to give them an arty feel. 'I love to work with reclaimed textiles for many reasons,' Dornan says. 'I see beauty in items that have been well loved, because they tell a story. Extending their lifespan keeps them out of landfills and gives them a role in making the textile industry more sustainable.'

Dornan has established two separate fashion labels, but the synergy between them enables them to be combined to create her signature look. 'Love in Tokyo', which is characterized by silk slip dresses, wrap skirts and camisoles in plain colours, is made to complement and be worn with 'Sheree Dornan'. The Sheree Dornan label includes one-off and limited-edition garments made from luxury silks and exclusive fabrics. Both labels are designed and produced in and around Fremantle, near Perth in Western Australia, where Dornan's Love in Tokyo boutique is situated. 'My labels are different from most others in the fashion industry, which produce clothing at a fast pace and use mass-production methods.' Dornan says, 'I don't use mass-produced textiles and I prefer to create limited editions and special one-off pieces. Using reclaimed textiles to make contemporary designs gives them a timeless quality. Each one is handcrafted and has the potential to become a future heirloom.'

According to Dornan, the textiles she creates are typically described as 'rescued, reworked and reclaimed'. Her prints are usually produced in small runs, and made by transferring digital prints onto silks and organic cotton. 'The unique garments I create are typically either from my limited-edition print designs or embellished with pieces of reclaimed fabrics, vintage embroidery and antique beading reworked into new designs,' Dornan explains. Many of the reclaimed items Dornan uses originated in Asia and Europe before being exported to Australia, giving her garments an exotic element.

Dornan's starting point is often finding ways to prolong the life of a vintage textile. 'When I use fragile old fabrics I fuse them onto silk organza backings and reinforce them with stitching to keep them from falling apart, Dornan explains. 'I may start with a piece of reclaimed fabric and marry it together with new fabrics to create the new garment which can have hand-embellished details. Some of my textiles are block-printed using reclaimed Indian woodblocks, then over-dyed by hand to create a desired finish. My jewellery range is created similarly, using old embroideries, metallic vintage mesh, vintage fabrics and adding beading and other found objects. You could say my work is about constant evolution.'

'The Bird and the Kimono' fashion collection featured dresses made from limited-edition silk twill fabrics digitally printed with four different print designs. Dornan draped a rectangle of the fabric over a mannequin to create the

ALL IMAGES / Fabric scraps are never thrown away in Dornan's studio. Off-cuts and selvedges are stitched with leftover thread and embroidered with haberdashery pieces to create embellishments.

dress without any off-cuts or fabric waste. 'Using vintage finds reduces textile waste, but so can conscientious workmanship,' Dornan says. 'Fabric can be draped and cut in an efficient, economical way that minimizes off-cuts, and hence waste. Digital design processes and digital printing use fewer resources than traditional methods.'

Each of Dornan's designs balances luxury and economy, and fuses elegance with understated beauty. Although Dornan never set out to establish sustainable fashion labels, her approach to textile design and initiatives to minimize waste have created exemplary methods of conserving resources without compromising appearance, colour or style.

ABOVE / Dornan's textile designs are used in a wide range of applications. Printed onto interior textiles, they make striking upholstery and eye-catching lampshades. Mounted on stretcher strips, they add an artistic element to the interior.

RIGHT / Earth tones are often combined with colours from nature to create colourways that are soothing to the eye, yet energetic and uplifting too.

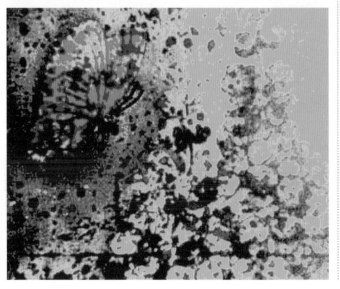

ABOVE / Some of Dornan's prints can be described in terms of their romanticism and mystery. This motif, with its floral print and dark background, reveals a neo-Gothic dimension to her work.

RIGHT / Dornan strives to achieve a balance between print design, functionality, texture and colour. Whether adapting a vintage textile for use today or creating a new design for her collection, sustainable principles underpin her work.

Sheree Dornan's work with reclaimed textiles keeps them out of landfills and gives them a new life, making the textile industry more sustainable as a result.

BELOW / Dornan takes a painterly approach to pattern design. As she designs textiles with a layered tableaux, she creates motifs that tell a story.

OPPOSITE & FAR RIGHT / Dornan's pattern repeats are derived from a variety of inspirations and techniques. Some prints are created by photographing objects or scanning vintage fabrics, creating a design to be digitally printed in short runs.

OPPOSITE, BELOW RIGHT / Flora and fauna feature in many of Dornan's motifs. Renderings of plants and wildlife may be drawn using a style or colour palette associated with the Far East, lending an exotic element.

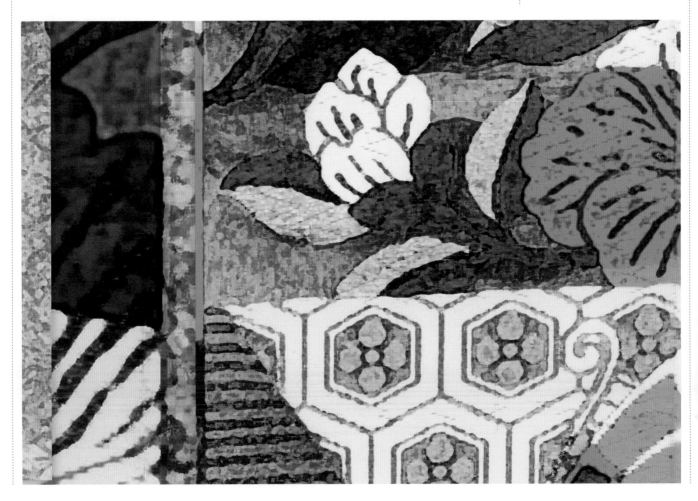

THIS PAGE / Garments designed for The Bird and the Kimono collection were crafted individually by draping silk twill fabric rather than cutting and sewing it. Each garment was created to showcase the print design and is softly shaped to fit the body.

ABOVE & RIGHT / Sheree's digitally printed designs shown above are inspired by vintage kimonos, right.

THIS PAGE / The heady glamour of the roaring twenties and the elegance of the pre-war period are inspirations for Dornan. She uses sequins, embroidery and shiny beads to recreate the mystery and romance of bygone eras.

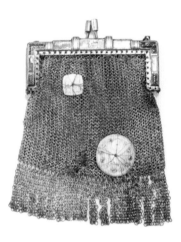

ALL IMAGES / In Dornan's hands, vintage textiles, discarded trims and lost buttons are a precious resource. The purses shown here are pieces she has collected from antique shops and markets, darning them with metallic copper and gold threads and adding embellishments such as beads and vintage watch faces.

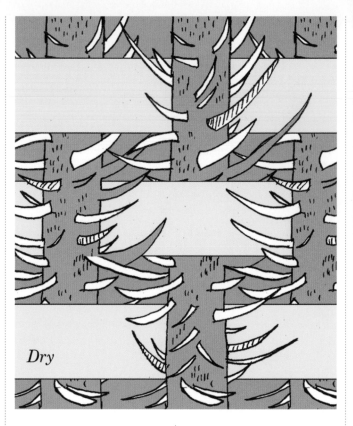

Dry

VERONIKA KAPSALI

New methods of sustainability have the potential to radically reinvent the ways that textiles are designed, manufactured and consumed. One of these is the science of biomimicry (from the Greek *bios*, meaning 'life', and *mimesis*, meaning 'to imitate'), a discipline that emulates processes found in the natural world by using technology to recreate them. London-based textile designer Veronika Kapsali was one of the first practitioners to research biomimetic textiles with a view to heightening the performance of garments. Today, she is a founding director of MMT Textiles, a design studio and lab established to create biomimetic systems for use in textiles and clothing.

While carrying out research for her PhD, Kapsali developed an adaptive textile, inspired by the way that moisture can induce shape changes in many types of plant structures. 'The textile works the opposite way that conventional natural fibres do,' Kapsali explains. 'Fibres such as wool and cotton swell as they absorb moisture, which reduces the porosity of the textiles they comprise. The system I created becomes more porous as it absorbs moisture.' The textile that resulted could be used in applications such as sportswear, where perspiration would cause the network of fibres to expand and open, enabling moisture to move away from the skin and onto the surface of the fabric, where it quickly evaporates.

The inspiration behind Kapsali's adaptive textile was the pine cone, which opens to release its seeds during dry conditions to allow the wind to disseminate

Damp

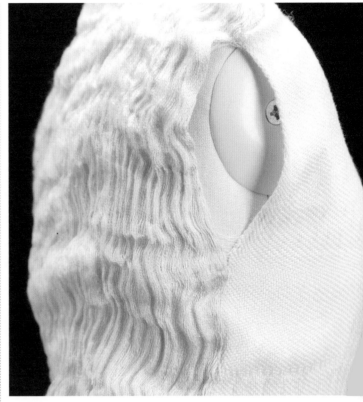

ABOVE RIGHT / Kapsali's moisture-control system heightens the performance of the garments by keeping the wearer comfortable and dry. This prototype shows how yarns are carefully woven in specific positions to create a biomimetic structure.

LEFT / When Kapsali applies her textile methodology to garments, she conceives openings such as necklines and armholes to be vents for cooling and drying the wearer.

the seeds far away; if they were dispersed in damp conditions they would likely germinate too close to the seed-bearing tree and have to compete with it for resources. 'I could see that the pine cone's system could be applied to clothing in order to prevent the build up of moisture,' Kapsali says. 'Such a fabric could make wearers more comfortable when they have to wear warm winter coats in heated environments, such as trains and shops.' Kapsali is developing her adaptive system to perform so efficiently that it regulates the temperature around the wearer to the degree that they may not need several layers of clothing in winter. 'Right now we rely on a modular system of cold-weather clothing to keep us comfortable,' Kapsali explains. 'We add layers to insulate ourselves when cold, and remove them to ventilate

our bodies when we get too warm. My technology shows that an adaptive textile could be used to make a single, temperature-regulating garment, which would redefine the modular approach to clothing that we take today.'

Kapsali has also written about the biomimetic application known as the 'Lotus Effect'. Leaves of the waterborne lotus plant demonstrate water-repellency and self-cleaning properties, which researchers attribute to layers of wax-like crystals that cover the surface of each leaf. 'I first saw the lotus' surface reproduced in a masonry paint that would self-clean every time it rains or gets sprayed with water,' Kapsali said. 'I could see that the technology has applications in the textile sector as a fabric finish that delivers

water-, stain- and dirt-resistant properties to clothing without affecting the appearance, drape or feel of the cloth.'

'No wash' garments are sustainable in several ways, as minimal energy and resources are required to clean them. Kapsali is developing a method of creating fully formed garments from woven textiles without cutting and sewing the fabric, which also minimizes textile waste. 'Nature is full of structural hierarchies,' Kapsali explains. 'I can apply that principle to the design of textiles to engineer shape into a textile structure through combinations of yarns and finishes that are placed in different positions. The tension and give between them can be engineered to pull the garment taut in some places and make it loose in others.'

Kapsali's biomimetic approach is establishing a new forum for smart textile systems. While most smart systems currently rely on temperature to trigger a change, Kapsali's lessons from nature revealed that moisture, in the form of humidity, perspiration and steam, can be equally effective. 'By building a cross-disciplinary relationship between science and textile design we have created a smart textile that doesn't need a technical language to program it,' Kapsali says. 'At this point we can make

ABOVE & RIGHT / The pine cone provided the inspiration behind Kapsali's biomimetic textile. These illustrations show pine cones that have opened after absorbing enough moisture through their shells to release seeds.

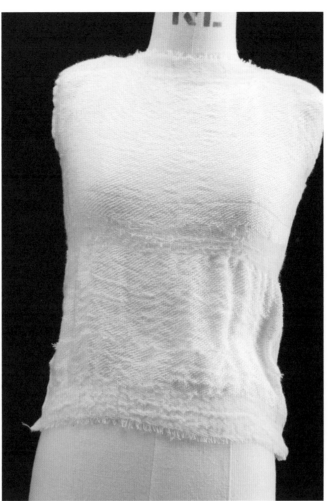

LEFT & BELOW / The prototypes Kapsali is currently developing use fibres such as wool and cotton, which swell as they absorb moisture, reducing porosity. Kapsali's system enables the fibres to become more porous as they absorb moisture, enabling moisture to move away from the skin and onto the surface of the fabric, where it evaporates quickly.

Veronika Kapsali creates biomimetic systems for use in textiles and clothing. Her fabric designs imitate nature to boost performance and use fewer resources.

INNOVATION

No longer produced solely for practical needs or decorative purposes alone, textiles are playing an important role in taking technology forwards. Fabrics created with colour-changing surfaces, light-emitting fibres and animated motifs are heralding a new generation of surface technology, which is becoming widespread in architecture and product design. Textiles with interactive capabilities and communication technology provide technology pliant enough to wear on the body and to fashion into soft objects. When embedded with electronics, textiles can be enhanced with robotics and computation capacities that enable them to move and change shape.

Innovation describes more than new methods and fresh ideas; it also describes the new applications found for traditional materials. The technologically enhanced fabrics being developed today have complex surfaces, relying on textures, embellishments and reactive surfaces to conceal the mechanics and devices embedded within them. Many can morph into new shapes and still revert to their original design, and provide a dynamic means of interacting with the spaces surrounding them.

As fresh approaches imbue textile design with extravagance and imagination, they also make space for brilliant colours, rich textures, unexpected finishes and elaborate motifs. The combination of smart textiles and printing technologies developed by Kerri Wallace, for example, signal a fresh approach to sportswear fabrics as they

ABOVE / Because emotions and the tactile senses are inextricably linked, a fabric's texture, tactility and performance are a significant part of wearing clothes. Eun-Jeong Jeon's Trans-For-M-otion kinetic fabric reacts to the wearer's emotional states by automatically closing and opening around them.

RIGHT, CENTRE / Self-illuminating photonic fibres and colour-changing filaments can be integrated into many types of fabrics, enabling them to undergo a reversible colour change when exposed to sunlight, or emit light in the dark.

FAR RIGHT / As advanced fibres make fabrics more durable and stain-resistant, they also enable designers to create innovative textures, such as those shown here.

UNTIL RECENTLY, SPECIALIST knowledge of advanced materials and new technology was left to experts or scientists, but today many of those active in these fields are taking a collaborative approach. In the hands of textile designers, the new techniques, intelligent interfaces, sensory surfaces and smart substances being developed today are radically redefining the way fabrics are created. As a new generation of textile designers move forwards, the innovations they are pioneering are radically transforming traditional approaches. Now dynamic and interactive, textile practice is regarded as one of the richest areas of innovation in design today.

sense the wearer's body heat and cause colourways and patterns to change in response to it. Body heat can also be harnessed to create custom fabrics and whole garments, as the 3D thermal scanning systems and advanced computational strategies used by Skin Graph reveal.

Although light plays an essential role in textile design, its ability to function as a design device has not been recognized until recently. Kathy Schicker uses photonic technology to create light-reactive fibres and colour-changing fabrics. Similarly, Aurélie Mossé transforms light into an energy source that provides power for micro-controllers embedded in interior surfaces, enabling them to change colour and texture. When principles of mechanization are applied to textile design, fabrics can be engineered to move and assume new forms. The textiles developed by Priti Veja are made with advanced materials and embedded with soft technological parts that enable them to move and assume new shapes. Jenny Leary also makes textiles that are capable of changing texture and shape, which she initiates by activating magnetic fields built within the fabric's structure.

As this section charts some of the most innovative methods and approaches gaining currency in the field today, it challenges the assumption that fabrics should be shaped by textile practice alone. Many of the works featured in the following texts promise to radically invent textile design, and as they do so, they also reveal its potential to influence other disciplines.

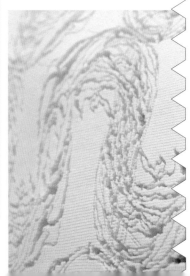

Concerns about personal security are generating a demand for protective clothing, which urban dwellers want to appear as tailored and chic as the rest of their wardrobes. The No Contact Jacket, shown here, was designed with an outer surface that deploys an electrical charge which can protect the wearer from attackers.

ADAM WHITON & YOLITA NUGENT

Body technology is a hot topic at the Massachusetts Institute of Technology's (MIT) Media Lab, where fibres, textiles and garments are radically transforming what the human body can achieve. Adam Whiton, a researcher and PhD candidate at MIT, has developed some of the most shocking technology the Media Lab has released to date: he designs textiles embedded with electronics, robotics and computation capacities, aiming to find solutions for some of the issues women are faced with today.

One of Whiton's projects equips women with the means to fend off attackers, in the form of a wearable textile system that emits an electrical charge when touched. Whiton teamed up with fashion designer Yolita Nugent to make the system wearable, resulting in a chic jacket that delivers a shock strong enough to make attackers lose their grip and back off, allowing the wearer to get away.

Suitably named the 'No Contact Jacket', the garment contains conductive fibres such as Aracon from DuPont, which is an Aramid fibre clad in silver. The conductive fibres are woven and stitched into pathways throughout the jacket that disperse the electrical charge across the jacket's surface when constricted by an attacker's grip. The jacket is comprised of a layered system that includes a liner, electrical insulating layer, the conductive/electrified layer and a waterproof outer shell. The liner protects the wearer from the electrical charge, and a key-activated switch triggers the system to deploy the electrical charge if constricted, or deactivates it so that the wearer can interact with others as normal.

Whiton and Nugent are also developing technological systems that detect and record physical violence. The systems are conceived as wearable computers that can be integrated into clothing to sense and record physical blows to the body. As the technology documents the blows the wearer receives, they quantify the degree of physical abuse the wearer has been subjected to. 'The system contains fabric-based pressure sensors that gauge the patterns of blows to the wearer's body and measure their intensity', Whiton explains. 'The system could record the cumulative history of the wearer's abuse, while gathering data that could be used by social psychologists.'

The system is made with composite materials known as Quantum Tunnelling Composites (QTCs), which consist of metals and nonconducting elastomeric binders bonded to the garment's fibres. The materials are activated by pressure, becoming electrically conductive when they come into contact with one another, creating links that enable the electrons to record the extent and duration of the force.

Another form of abuse Whiton and Nugent are tracking is that of violent shaking. Abusers have been reported to grasp the victim by the arms or shoulders and shake them vigorously, inflicting physical and emotional trauma without leaving marks on the skin. 'This violent action results in bilateral oscillating forces on both the left and

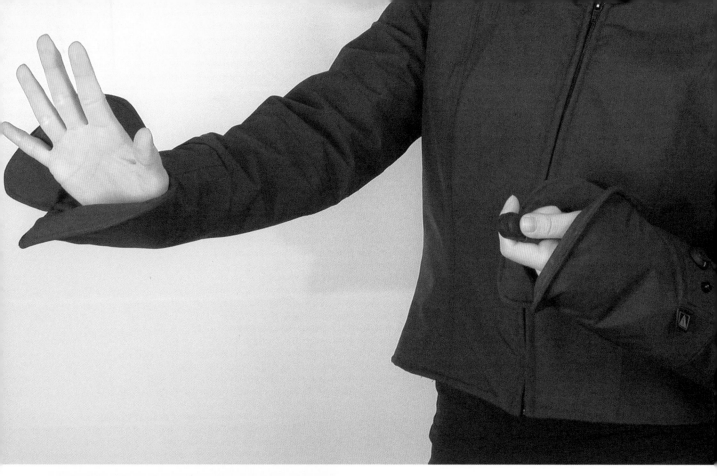

right upper arm areas,' Whiton explains. 'These characteristics are distinctive, because we do not usually observe forces like these during normal everyday activity. The system makes it possible for the data from the abuse to be viewed in real time, allowing the victim to receive help immediately.' The data the system records can be archived or distributed to the proper authorities for later legal or medical requirements.

As Whiton's and Nugent's textile-based detection systems become wearable, they make it easier to identify physical abuse. Although computer systems cannot actually record the feelings of pain and emotional suffering a victim feels, they can detect abuse sufficiently to alert medical practitioners and law enforcement personnel. Although Whiton's and Nugent's systems are still in development, they show how textile-based technologies are paving the way for a new field of future investigation.

RIGHT & BELOW / Combining conductive fibres and insulators into a composite textile layer with a battery-powered energy source, Whiton and Nugent created a unique protective material. The jacket's electric charge is activated/deactivated by a hand-held switch, shown here.

OPPOSITE / Whiton and Nugent position wearable technologies in key positions on the body in order to document any physical trauma experienced by the wearer. The garment shown here can record physical pressure, then transfer the data to a computer or smart phone for analysis. It can also operate in real time.

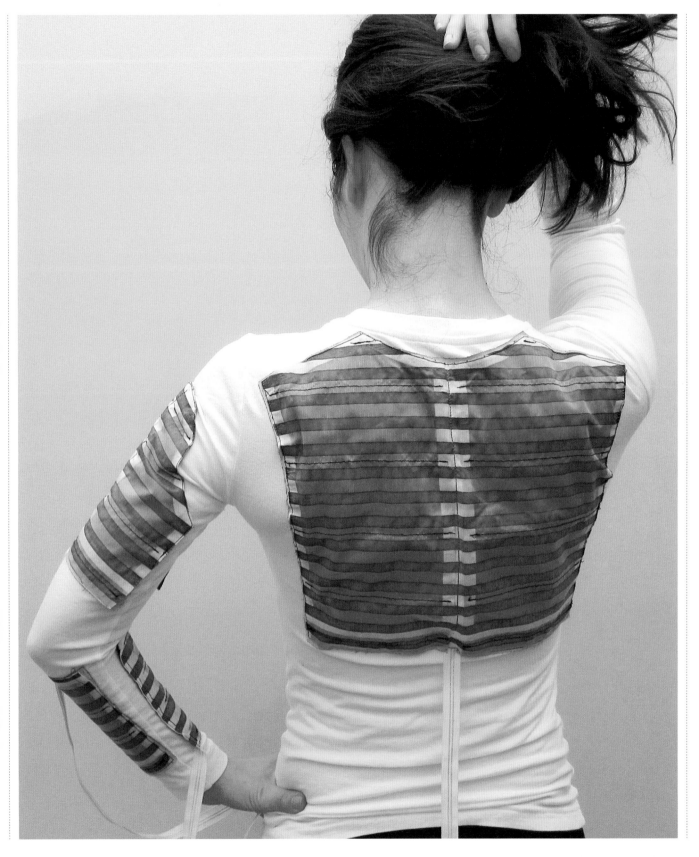

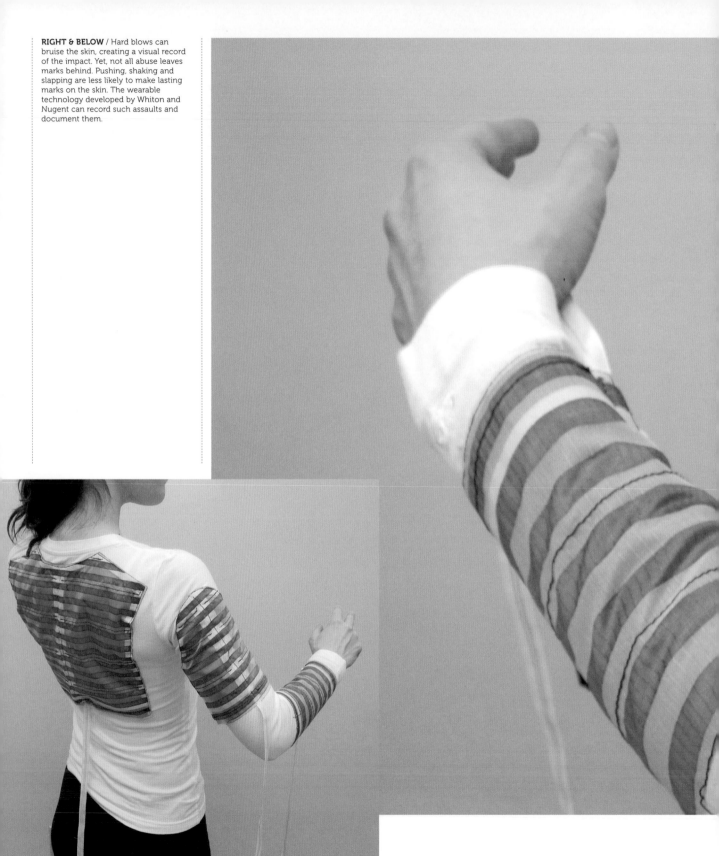

RIGHT & BELOW / Hard blows can bruise the skin, creating a visual record of the impact. Yet, not all abuse leaves marks behind. Pushing, shaking and slapping are less likely to make lasting marks on the skin. The wearable technology developed by Whiton and Nugent can record such assaults and document them.

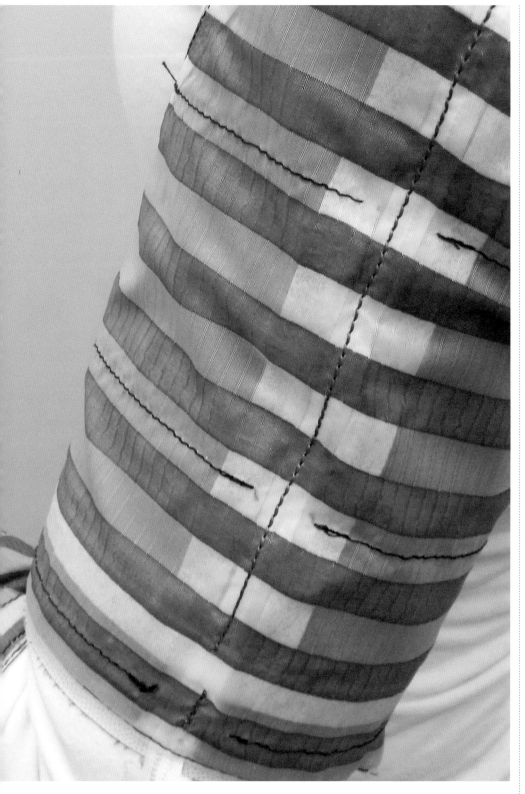

Adam Whiton and Yolita Nugent designed a textile that emits an electric charge when touched. The shock makes attackers lose their grip and back off, enabling the wearer to get away.

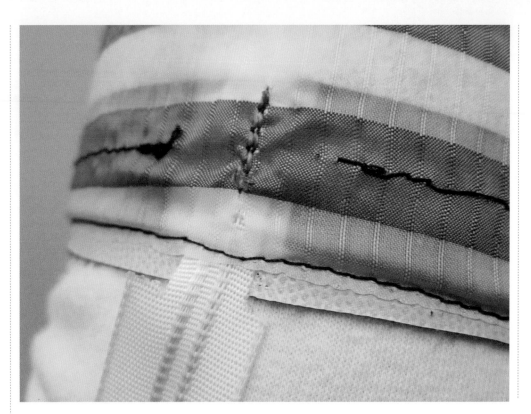

THIS PAGE / Sensors and circuitry are embedded within fabric to create a diagnostic system that is soft, flexible and wearable. After a period of wear, the garment is connected to a computer where information about the force it has recorded is downloaded and analysed. Data plots of the force, such as the one shown on the right, enable technicians to differentiate between the pressure of a hug and the force of a blow.

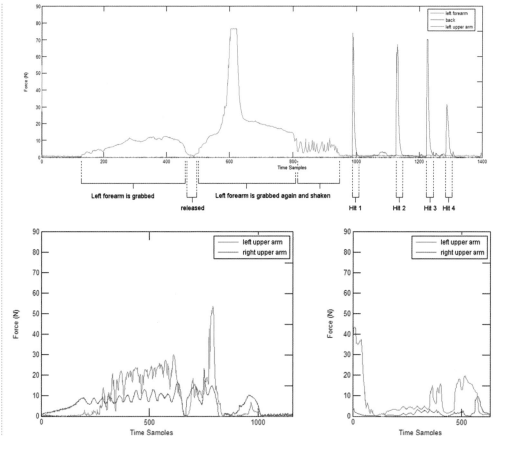

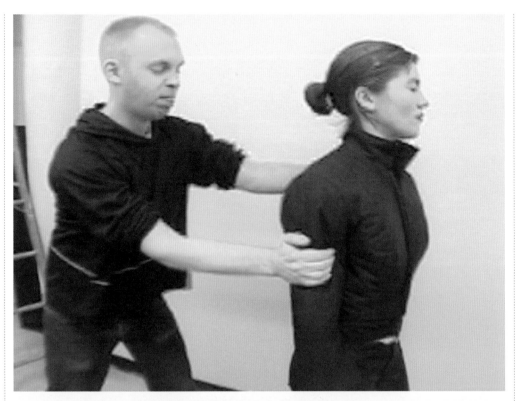

LEFT / The electrical charge emitted by the jacket is between 30-50kv. The charge is not strong enough to knock the attacker to the ground, but makes them back off immediately. The demonstrator shown in this test described the shock as 'having your palm slapped hard with a ruler, so hard that it stings all the way up to your shoulder'.

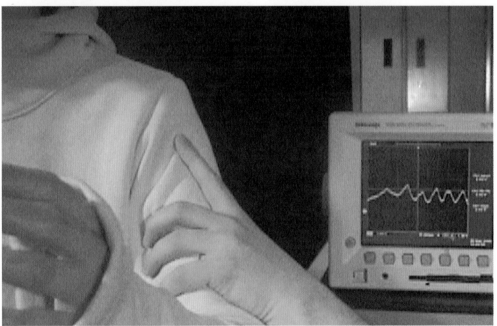

BELOW / Here, a demonstrator squeezes the wearer's arm intermittently while sensor force output is viewed and analyzed using an oscilloscope.

AURÉLIE MOSSÉ

Future worlds will be based on transition, and textile design, like architecture and interiors, will reflect the ever-changing nature of the fast-paced lives we will lead. Built structures will be perceived as fluid rather than fixed, and technologized textiles will enable designers to create fabric forms that promote shifting relationships between user and object. Aurélie Mossé, a French textile designer and researcher, is pioneering fresh potentials for textile forms in this exciting new area. As she investigates the role that self-actuated textiles can play in the interiors of the future, Mossé is creating designs that reveal a new synergy between textiles, material science and biomimicry.

Mossé first gained international acclaim when design magazine *Azure* chose her as a front runner in design in 2010, including her among the 25 young designers whose work is changing the shape of things to come. The magazine described Mossé as a 'textile evolutionist', choosing the term because it summarizes her technique of combining fibres with natural phenomena so that exchanges will evolve between them over time.

Mossé's point of departure from conventional textile design is her fascination with shape-morphing materials, particularly those that respond to light or reconfigure into new forms. As a part of her PhD research at CITA (an institute within the Royal Danish Academy of Fine Arts' architecture faculty) and TFRC (textile futures research centre at Central Saint Martins, London) she created an interdisciplinary consortium to explore the potential of shape-morphing textiles for a range of architectural and interior surfaces. Carrying out research in the field of electroactive and light-responsive polymers has led to several collaborations between Mossé and the Philips Design 'Probes' team in the Netherlands.

One of Mossé's investigations into architectural surfaces explores the potential to create 'minimum energy structures' that reconfigure into new forms. The structures are based on pre-stretching a chain of elastomers that are overlaid onto a flexible frame. When an electric current is applied, the structure is triggered to change form, allowing actuation to occur as it morphs back to its original shape. Mossé adapted the technology to create the ceiling surface she calls *Reef*, which is a reactive architectural membrane based on dielectric elastomers capable of effecting a three-dimensional change of shape. '*Reef* is composed of an "archipelago" of electroactive modules that sense wind intensity and direction,' Mossé explains. 'The modules change shape accordingly, constantly reconfiguring the surface as they do so.' The system relies on a wind sensor coupled to a microcontroller that induces the actuation of the modules as it transmits information between an inner layer and the exterior surface.

Reef works similarly to the solar-responsive 'Photovoltaic Mashrabiya' composite textile membrane that Mossé is developing today. The design mimics the appearance of the carved wooden latticework characteristic of traditional

Arabic architecture; the membrane converts light into electricity to create the energy required to make it fold and unfold according to the level of sunshine it detects. The membrane acts as a barrier that minimizes the amount of solar heat and sunlight that pass through a window. Mossé used the same principles to create a prototype of a light-responsive wallpaper that harnesses the sunlight that reaches interior walls. Called 'Constellation Wallpaper', the design is made of two layers of paper. The first layer transforms the sunlight into electricity, and the second layer performs like a battery to store the electricity. Flaps in the wallpaper surface open up when the wallpaper is accumulating energy, and then close when the power source is spent.

As Mossé makes interior design more responsive, the premise that a fixed surface should constitute the basis of design will be irrevocably reversed. Shape-shifting materials, programmable surfaces, technological interfaces and labile components will transfigure everyday objects into interactive tools for dynamic lifestyles.

ABOVE & RIGHT / The structures that constitute *Reef* (shown on the previous page) are based on pre-stretching elastic materials that Mossé overlaid onto flexible structures, such as those shown here. The structure can be triggered to change form by the application of an electric current. Once the current is switched off, the design morphs back to its original shape.

LEFT & BELOW / Although Mossé's *Reef* installation may appear to be high-tech, the inspiration behind it was Nature itself. Mossé created the installation to explore how adaptive minimum-energy structures can make an interior more in harmony with nature. The modules react to airflow in the interior, opening and closing as they sense the circulation of air.

LEFT & BELOW / Mossé is among the first textile designers to explore the potentials of dielectric elastomers, which are essentially plastic materials that change shape when an electric current is applied. The electrical charge can be applied in such a way that the elastomers contract in the direction of the electrical charge while expanding in the other direction, making it possible to control their movement.

ABOVE & TOP RIGHT / Mossé's knitted fabrics, shown here, were created to explore how traditional methods of interconnecting fibres can be adapted for contemporary textiles. Mossé's practice explores many such interconnections to create new methods of conducting electrical currents and transmitting digital data.

RIGHT / The award-winning *Ice Fern* textile sculpture was co-designed by Mossé and CITA colleagues Karin Bech, Mette Ramsgaard Thomsen and Martin Tamke, created as part of the architectural knitting workshop at Shankar University organized by Mette and Ayelet Karmon. *Ice Fern* was created to explore new applications of the Gecko textile, a nano-coated material that mimics the adhesive ability of the gecko lizard. The textile was awarded first prize in the Gecko: Think Forward Competition organized by Création Baumann, a Swiss manufacturer of interior textiles.

THIS PAGE / Mossé created a
collection of domestic surfaces she
called '[Extra]ordinary furniture',
which includes the 'mille-feuille' table
surface, shown here. The tabletop was
made from materials such as Tecofoil,
cardboard and a synthetic paper called
Yupo, designed to be peeled away,
layer by layer, to reveal a new surface
underneath. The peeled layers can be
re-used to decorate other surfaces.

Aurélie Mossé investigates the role that self-actuated textiles can play in the interior, creating designs that reveal new synergy between textiles, materials and biomimicry.

EUNJEONG JEON

From her base in Western Australia, Korean designer and researcher Eunjeong Jeon engineers wearable fabrics to have sensing, adapting and reacting capabilities. Embedded with sensory technology, Jeon's textiles move and change shape. They respond to the wearer's actions by changing texture and reconfiguring their position on the body.

The kinaesthetic experiences that fabrics have when worn make them dynamic and interactive as they flex and bend on the body. Jeon's research is tracking the extent to which fabrics can also reflect the space around them, as they move in response to how the wearer engages with the environments around them. 'My research investigates the roles that textiles play in women's experiences of their bodies and the spaces around them,' Jeon explains. 'Human actions and perceptions of the spaces they move within evoke different emotions. To create my fabrics, I develop designs based on movement-based interactions that respond to emotions. By using wool as a base material within which I can incorporate technology, I design textiles that interact with the wearer.'

Jeon calls the project 'Trans-For-M-otion': this research is linked to the ARC Linkage project 'Innovative Solutions for Wool Garment Comfort though Design' (ID: LP0775433), in conjunction with the Wooldesk at DAFWA (Department of Agriculture and Food, Western Australia). In the

LEFT / The textiles Jeon designs have complex surfaces and contain reactive technologies. This fabric illuminates in response to the wearer's movements.

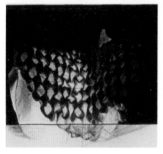

ABOVE & RIGHT / Jeon's Trans-For-M-otion project includes textiles that react to the way the body moves. Transitional spaces, such as airports and train stations, cue the textiles to create soft enclosures around the wearer.

course of her research, Jeon has developed prototypes that react to the way the body moves as it travels through transitional spaces, such as airports and roads. 'I chose places where we encounter sudden temperature changes, noise and pollution, as well as stress and even crime,' Jeon says. 'My prototypes are made to respond to these spaces and they have performances capabilities that make the wearer feel more comfortable when inhabiting those spaces.'

The prototypes were developed in conjunction with women who Jeon interviewed about their experiences of transitional spaces. Many of them gave accounts of feeling insecure at times. 'My textiles are designed to detect feelings such as fear and react by closing around the wearer to foster a greater sense of security.' The textiles contain small cells that trap air. When positioned at the neck or along the shoulders of a garment, they reinforce the sense of protection the design affords. 'The air unit structures can create a garment that works like a cushion,' Jeon explained. 'It helps the wearer protect their body.'

Embedding the garment with LED light technology enhances its function as a mask to hide, protect, reassure and distort the self when the wearer is in danger of attack. 'The wearer can move the garment themselves to position it in a way that makes them feel protected,' Jeon explains. 'Some of the women I interviewed wanted to be able to disguise themselves or hide their identity, so I designed the garment to also be pulled upwards so that the collar can conceal part of the face.' Jeon is further experimenting with embedded sensors that monitor the wearer's muscle tension, breathing, heart rate and body temperature to detect when they feel uncomfortable. As the garment is triggered to close around the wearer, the shape of its silhouette relates directly to the wearer's sense of emotional and physical well-being.

Apart from Trans-For-M-otion's protective function, the textile is also able to facilitate personal expression. 'The textile is an interactive tool,' Jeon says. 'It can be worn in a playful way. It was interesting to note that the women I interviewed described how garment forms could foster a sense of security in an insecure situation. Yet, when I observed how they wore the textile, I could clearly see how much the women enjoyed manipulating it and interacting with it.'

Trans-For-M-otion's unique sensory abilities enable it to simulate a wide range of responses, making Jeon a leader in the emerging field of sensory textiles. As a new generation of fabric unfolds, the complex surfaces, sophisticated structures and reactive technologies they feature promise to transform how garments are made and worn. In future, fashion textiles may do more than just cover the body. They may even provide the wearer with the means of interacting with the spaces surrounding them.

ABOVE & RIGHT / Jeon used wool as a base material for these designs. The wool fabric was structured in innovative ways to create tiny apertures that move in response to technological components integrated in the fabric.

OPPOSITE PAGE, MAIN IMAGE / Jeon's fabrics are based on the study of movement and shaped by textile design. She documents the behaviour of volunteers to identify how the body senses, adapts and reacts under stressful conditions, then designs the textile to make movements that soothe the wearer in those situations.

OPPOSITE PAGE, INSET / When triggered to protect the shoulders and head, Jeon's fabric creates a personal enclosure that moves with the body.

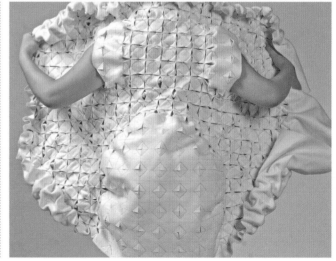

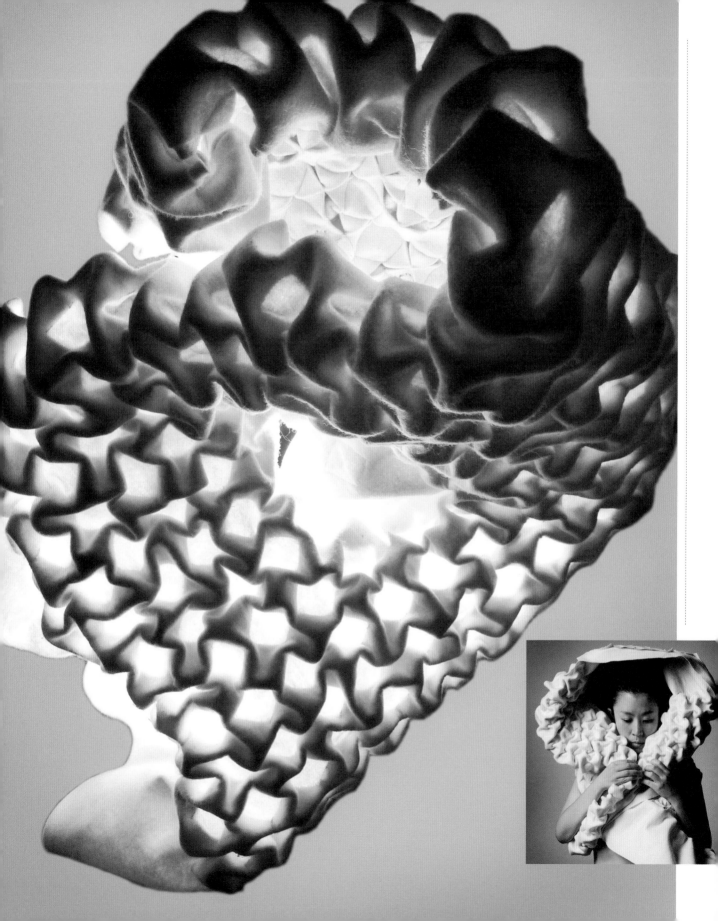

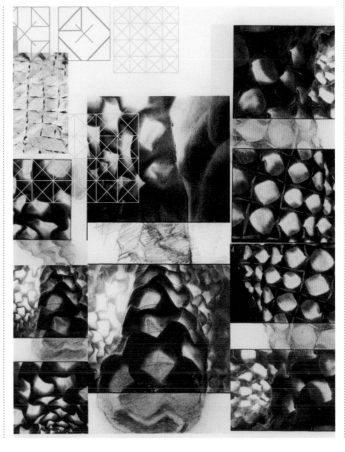

ABOVE & RIGHT / Jeon engineers her fabrics to have sensing, adapting and reacting capabilities. She calculates precisely where the embedded technology should be placed in order to make the textiles move and change shape.

LEFT / Protection and security are themes that Jeon explores in her textile designs. By using dense fabrics or creating intricately structured textiles, Jeon creates protective enclosures for wear on the body.

BELOW / Interaction is the essence of Jeon's work. Her designs are created with the wearers in mind, who enjoy manipulating and interacting with the fabrics they wear.

Eunjeong Jeon's fabrics are based on movement-based interactions that respond to emotions.

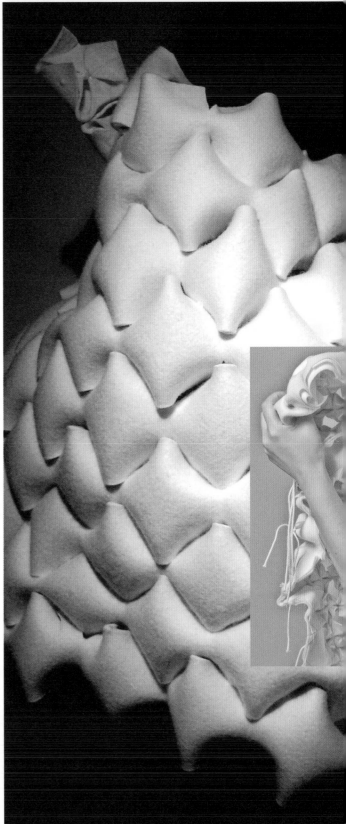

RIGHT / Although Jeon's textiles are richly-structured and embedded with technology, they are soft to the touch and comfortable to wear.

BELOW / Unique surface textures and custom-fits characterize Jeon's designs, giving them an edgy fashion aesthetic.

THIS PAGE / The textile's air cells can be positioned at the garment's neck or along the shoulders to reinforce the sense of protection the textile offers. The air cells work like a cushion to absorb and diffuse impacts and blows.

ABOVE LEFT & ABOVE RIGHT /
Jeon embeds garments with LED
light technology to give additional
functionality. The LEDs can highlight
the structure to create dramatic
contrasts, as shown here.

RIGHT / Integrated LEDs give the
wearer scope to create temporary
changes in the textile's surface. They
can trigger certain colours to appear,
or create a kaleidoscope effect.

TOP / Illuminating garments can enhance the wearer's sense of protection. If facing danger or threatened, the LEDs can be triggered to pulsate to attract attention or signal for help.

ABOVE / Jeon's designs remain at the prototype stage while she fine-tunes their performance and functionality.

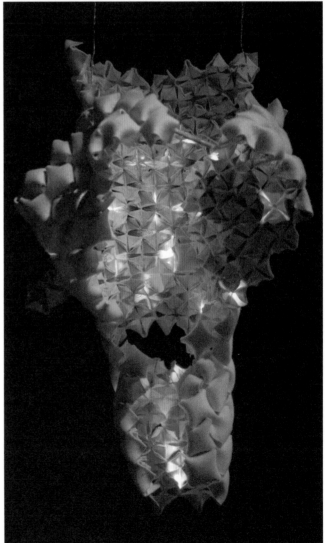

RIGHT / In addition to integrating LEDs into her fabrics, Jeon is experimenting with embedded sensors that monitor the wearer's muscle tension, breathing, heart rate and body temperature to detect when they feel uncomfortable.

GIADA DAMMACCO

The point at which the Equator (0 degrees latitude) and the Prime Meridian (0 degrees longitude) intersect creates a coordinate of zero degrees. When the same position is projected into space, it reaches the First Point of Aries, the reference point from where navigational stars are mapped. With their sights set on reaching the stars, the Italian research lab Grado Zero Espace (zero degree space) named themselves after this celestial coordinate. Established to pioneer space industry applications for materials, textiles and technologies, they literally aim for the stars. In the ten years that they have been established, GZE (as Grado Zero Espace is usually called) have developed a range of groundbreaking fabrics that take textile innovation to a higher level.

As GZE broaden horizons for terrestrial technology, Giada Dammacco, the company's design director, explores fresh directions for textile research. Together with a team of product designers and textile experts, Dammacco develops complex textile structures, which are often endowed with mechanical abilities. Research typically starts at the fibre level, where the yarn itself is manipulated and given specialist finishes. Dammacco handles technologically advanced materials such as thermo-active alloys and elastic polymers, but also works with low-tech natural fibres derived from kapok, peat, nettles bushes and cypress trees. Dammacco and her team derived a means of manipulating the shape memory alloy Nitinol to invent Oricalco, the first ever orthogonally woven textile, and subsequently used the fabric to make a 'self-ironing' shirt. Joint research into the potential of spider silk carried out with the University of California resulted in a lightweight, durable fabric derived from spider silk, that proved to be three times stronger than Kevlar.

Computer-generated geometric models and algorithm software packages are among the tools that Dammacco uses to develop her designs. 'Computer software makes it possible to analyse a material's thermal, mechanical and engineering properties,' Dammacco explains, 'enabling us to develop new types of textiles, as well as the means to fully test them. Each new fabric we create results from combining our textile skills with our engineering expertise.' Not only are GZE's textiles designed to have advanced performance capabilities, they are also made to absorb technological parts such as sensors, thermal-regulating systems, electroluminescent devices and conductive circuitry. 'Wearable technology is a one of our biggest research interests,' Dammacco says.

Fishing industry initiatives to enhance the protective clothing worn by fishermen sparked the Safe@Sea project, which resulted in new, 'intelligent' apparel that heightens the wearer's safety without compromising their work performance. 'We used new technical materials and developed communication software compatible with existing maritime transmission frequencies,' Dammacco says. 'The outfit that resulted senses when the wearer has fallen overboard and automatically inflates to keep them afloat.

The wearable technology relays a signal to the boat's engine, stopping it immediately. Emergency beacons are deployed in both the garment and the boat to attract help quickly.'

Working collaboratively with motorcycle clothing brand Spidi, GZE developed a wearable cooling system that helps the rider maintain a low body temperature in sweltering temperatures. Technology developed to cool astronauts travelling through solar temperatures was combined with satellite technology, micropumps and rehydration systems to create a base-layer-like garment. The system was also used to make cooling overalls for racing-car drivers and special helmets that simultaneously cool the wearer and deflect heat.

As Dammacco pushes the boundaries of wearable technology, she is pioneering new applications for electro-luminescent materials. GZE is adapting 'Re Light' technology, a light-emitting surface derived from electroactive nanocomposites, for application to textiles. Re Light is lightweight and fireproof, and able to withstand perforation, abrasion, torsion and compression. 'To describe it in the simplest terms, it can be applied to certain textiles like a coating,' Dammaco says. 'Yet, the textile remains soft and can be folded like any fashion fabric.' Dammacco believes that self-illuminating fabrics could be the next new horizon for textile design. 'Garments could then light up the wearer like a star,' she says, 'whether they are walking on Earth or carrying out a space walk in the sky.'

ABOVE / Hydro Jacket contains a thermal and moisture management layer based on a fabric coated with a water-absorbing polymer, developed especially for protective clothing. The outer shell deflects heat while the layer provides a thermal barrier that keeps heat away from the body.

LEFT / Working as chief designer at the Italian research lab Grado Zero Espace challenges Dammacco to develop textiles that will perform in outer space as well as they do on Earth. As she and the GZE team develop new textiles for use in space, they create processes that take textile innovation to a higher level on Earth.

BELOW / Developed by GZE, the Shape Memory Shirt is made from Oricalco fabric, the first shape memory woven textile. Composed of Nitinol, which is partially derived from titanium, it gives the shirt the ability to smooth itself out if creased. Nitinol can be pre-programmed to form a variety of shapes, then revert back to its starting point when heated. The Shape Memory Shirt has been included in the permanent collection of the Museum of Science and Industry in Chicago.

ABOVE / Spacesuits require a cooling layer to enable astronauts to withstand the high temperatures they experience when conducting space walks close to the Sun. The prototype garment shown here was commissioned by the European Space Agency. It contains more than 50 metres of plastic tubing that circulates cooling fluid around the wearer.

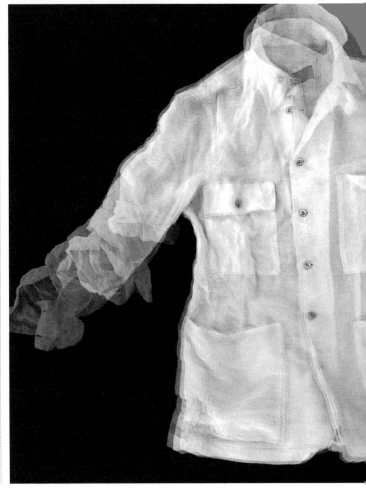

ABOVE / The S1 Suit is a protective suit designed for marine environments. Like the Oricalo Shirt, the shape memory fabric it is made from is soft and reacts to heat. The suit's glove is integrated with the sleeve, thereby avoiding the problem of losing a glove on deck during strong winds or stormy conditions.

OPPOSITE PAGE / Vectrasilk NT 32 is a high-performance yarn developed by GZE. The yarn combines the advanced performances of liquid crystal polymers with the tactility and shine of silk fibres, finding new use in the clothing sector. Vectrasilk NT 32 was developed for aerospace and sports applications.

Dammacco and her team handle advanced materials such as thermo-active alloys and elastic polymers, but also use low -tech fibres derived from peat, nettle bushes and cypress trees.

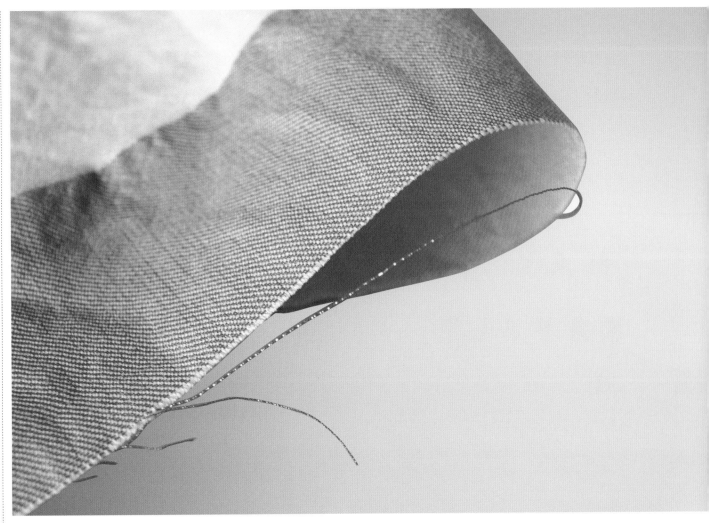

237 / GIADA DAMMACCO

RIGHT / The kinetic surface of Danny Rozin's 'Wooden Mirror' (1999), which uses live video data and servo motors to reflect the viewer and their background, was one of the inspirations that sparked Raffle's responsive surfaces.

OPPOSITE PAGE, TOP / Super Cilia Skin (SCS) could potentially be scaled up to create an exterior skin on skyscrapers that harnesses wind energy as it blows across a building's facade.

HAYES RAFFLE

Hayes Raffle is not a textile designer, but many of the tactile surfaces he creates mimic fabric in their structure, movement and folding action. Raffle invents sensory technology programmed with the potential for movement and actuation. When made into membranes, they form labile surfaces capable of sensing, reacting and moving in response to technological triggers. When combined with fabric substrates or fibrous materials, they can mimic conventional textiles in appearance, yet their performance is unlike any textile that has ever been made before.

Exploring the extent to which technological devices could be enhanced by the addition of a sensory interface, Raffle and his collaborators Mitchell Joachim and James Tichenor developed a technologized fabric membrane for use in a wide range of applications and environments. Currently at prototype stage, the membrane's surface is covered with an array of touch-sensitive, fibre-like actuators that respond to physical gestures. Known as 'Super Cilia Skin' (SCS), the membrane is constructed from a technologized surface that merges kinaesthetic input with tactile and visual output. 'Technically speaking, the membrane is a multi-modal digital interface that can be applied as a textile layer to create an interactive surface,' Raffle explains. 'The actuators that cover the surface are tiny, antenna-like projections that resemble a field of fibres. They are based on the cilia strands found in the cells of humans and many other organisms. Human

windpipes, for example, are lined by layers of undulating cilia, where they wick mucus and dirt particles up out of the lungs to be discharged by coughing.'

Clusters of cilia found in organisms can be thousand-fold: they are connected by a network of neural pathways that enable them to react as a single entity. As the cilia transfer information to each other through their neural network, they move in undulating, wave-like configurations. 'The Super Cilia Skin works similarly to the cilia found in living organisms,' explains Raffle. 'Its activity is triggered when it detects movement and touch in one area, which it then relays among a variety of separate, but interconnected, fibres to make the entire surface react the same way.' Although Raffle describes the SCS as a skin, its structure and performance are more akin to a textile membrane.

'SCS has the protective, sensory and tactile functions of fabric,' Raffle says. 'But as a digital, textural interface, it holds the potential to incorporate multiple applications and make complex switches between different data relays.' SCS's surface is constructed from an elastic membrane covered with an array of felt actuators called 'the cilia', which vary in size and scale and can be made from a range of materials. Whether aligned in a single row or grouped into large clusters, any changes caused by external forces are sensed by the magnetic field surrounding them and registered by the technology. If made into a tufted carpet, the cilia fibres would be interwoven in a networked system and linked to each other

RIGHT / SCS could be made into a tufted carpet by interweaving the cilia fibres within a networked system and linking them to each other via a computer interface. An SCS carpet in one room could display footsteps registered on an SCS surface in another area.

via a computer interface. When part of the carpet was brushed to smooth its surface, the sweeping movements would be registered throughout the rest of the carpet, automatically smoothing the entire surface. If made into clothing, small-scale cilia fibres could be engineered to respond to subtle movements created by the fingertips. An action such as touching one part of the garment would trigger the entire surface to react.

As the SCS system signposts a new direction for textiles, it also creates new possibilities for other industries. SCS can be increased in scale to create industrial-sized textiles for energy applications. Industrial-strength cilia could be engineered to harness wind power and convert it into electricity. 'The prototypes show that the movements of the cilia fibres can actually generate electrical power,' Raffle says, 'which could be used simultaneously or stored for later use. If we could scale up SCS to create an exterior skin on skyscrapers it could harness the wind energy that moves across the building's facade. Certain areas of the cilia could be isolated and programmed to respond to data transmission just as a digital billboard would, transforming parts of a building's facade into a self-powered display unit.' The potential for SCS to transform data transmission and design seems limitless. 'The prototypes are revealing a wide variety of applications for SCS,' Raffle says. 'Once SCS finds a market, it may revolutionize the way we think about surfaces today.'

ABOVE / SCS fibres are tiny, antenna-like projections that resemble a field of fibres. They are based on the cilia strands found in living organisms and fields of grasses found in nature.

RIGHT / Tim Prentice's 'Square Wind Frame' artwork gauges the velocity of the wind and triggers a surface of steel panels to respond to it. Its kinetic surface depicts changes around it in a manner similar to Raffle's SCS system.

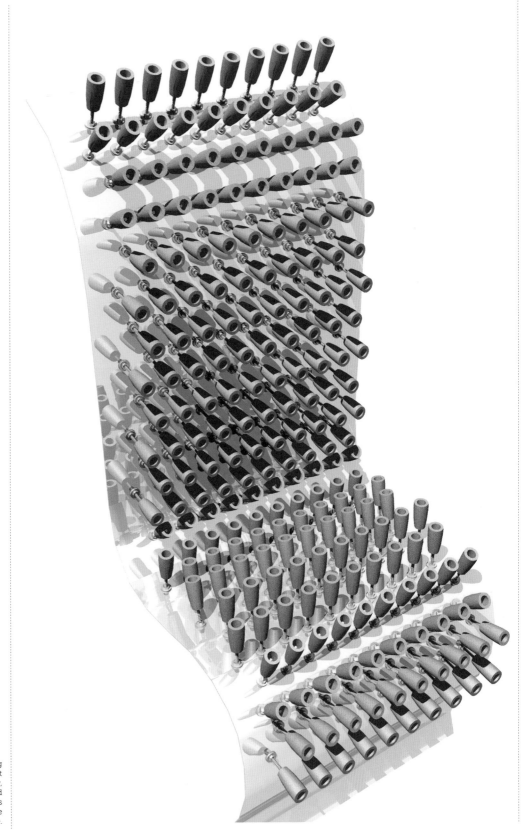

RIGHT / This conceptual rendering shows the individual actuators that form the SCS surface. Each is a tiny, antenna-like projection programmed to move in response to the actuators around it. As they do so, they enable the entire membrane to move as one.

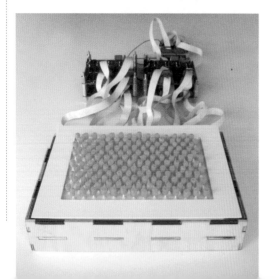

LEFT, ALL IMAGES / These SCS prototypes, placed on top of an actuated workbench, show how the array of touch-sensitive fibre-like actuators can 'draw' in response to magnetic fields. They are connected at the base and linked to technology that triggers them to move.

ABOVE / The actuators are designed to communicate with each other when interconnected. Covering them with a soft surface enhances the actuators' tactile appeal.

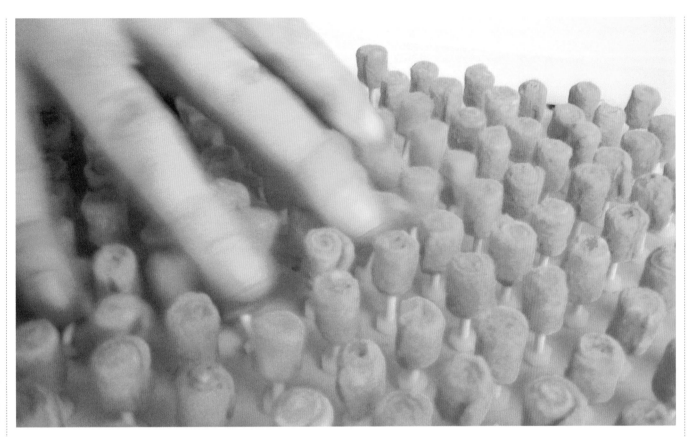

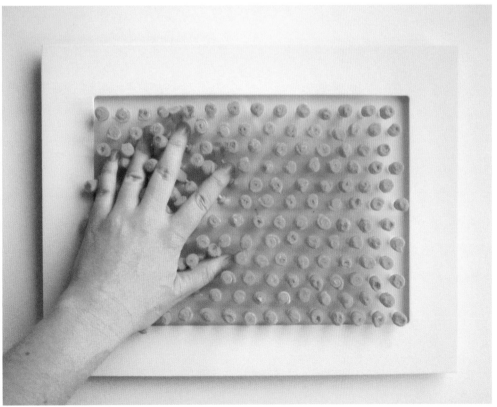

ABOVE & RIGHT / The SCS system uses colour and fibrous texture to engage sight and touch and facilitate remote interpersonal communication. Touch and gestures can become visible in the system and images can be felt as well as seen.

RIGHT / The Topobo building toy is a scalable, modular, actuated system that shares conceptual and material qualities with SCS. The pieces are designed to have a kinetic 'memory' that allows children to sculpt with movement and form.

BELOW / Soft toys, such as teddy bears, could potentially be covered with an SCS surface to make them interactive.

BELOW LEFT / These visual renderings were developed to explore the scale of the SCS and the potential to create industrial-sized SCS systems.

BOTTOM LEFT & RIGHT / These early prototypes were designed to mimic the clusters of cilia that occur naturally in organisms. Interconnecting them creates a network that enables them to react as a single entity.

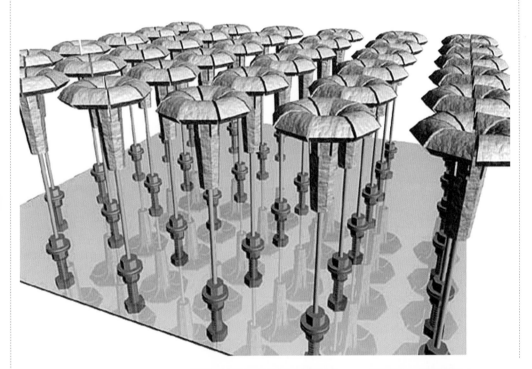

JENNY LEARY

RIGHT / Jenny Leary's work explores the relationship between magnetism and textiles. So far, Leary has discovered new methods of adhering textiles to walls and surfaces, and new ways of manipulating fashion fabrics.

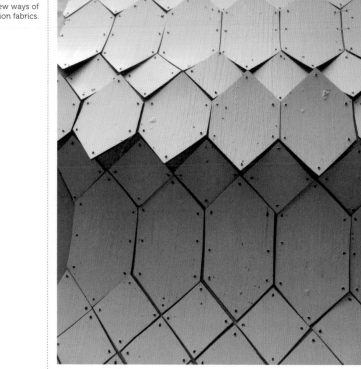

If Anton Mesmer, the eighteenth-century physician who treated his patients with magnets, were alive today, he'd probably decorate his walls with Jenny Leary's textiles. Mesmer believed that all living beings had magnetic fields coursing through them, which could be manipulated by magnetic objects placed close to the body. Similarly, Leary's innovative textiles include fabrics permeated with magnetic fields, which hold them permanently in place when fixed to walls and other types of interior surfaces.

From her studio in Los Angeles, the British-educated American designer is pioneering a range of magnetic textiles she calls 'Ferrofabric'. Although her practice is rooted in research, imagination is also a key component of Leary's design

ethos. 'Magnetic fields produce uncanny physical effects which spark our curiosity', she says. Although technological innovations enable Leary to adapt magnetic polarities for use in textile applications, traditional techniques continue to underpin her work. 'My materials and products are handcrafted, which may seem to make them distinct from technology,' Leary says. 'I think that the concept of technology is broad enough to include craft, especially when it is underpinned by scientific laws and can be explained in empirical terms.'

Leary realized that she was breaking new ground when she began exploring the possibilities that magnetic forces could have for textile-based experiments, but had no idea that it could lead to

a broad range of applications. 'The relationship between magnetism and textiles is very exciting, because it hasn't yet been explored to its full potential,' Leary says. 'I started by finding new ways of adhering textiles to walls and surfaces, but since then, I have discovered other ways of applying magnets to fabric design.' Leary is patenting a technique for embedding hidden images in textile surfaces that can only be revealed by a magnetic force. 'I have applied for a patent on a technique that uses magnetic force to create changes in the textile's surface, which can reveal new patterns and motifs.'

Ferrofabric wallcoverings are typically made of handcrafted textile squares magnetically imprinted with Leary's motifs or highly tactile textures. Each is a uniform size, and conceived as single unit of a larger pattern. The magnetic polarities between the fabric tiles and the wall surfaces they are mounted on holds them in place. The tiles peel off effortlessly and can be easily layered, reconfigured and reattached. 'When I see kids tinkering with the Ferrofabric wallcovering patterns for hours, I imagine that they'll be inspired to learn more about the forces of the physical universe. When Einstein was shown a compass at age five, he felt like he was witnessing a miracle, and never forgot it. The more opportunities we have to interact with strange materials, the better equipped we'll be to ask the questions of scientific investigation.'

As Leary continues to take Ferrofabric forwards, she regards it as an ongoing project to

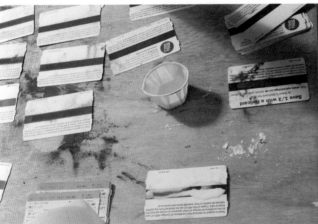

ABOVE / Leary regards magnetism as central to modern technologies. This transparent purse is printed with vestiges of the bank card it would normally contain, showing how textiles could encode magnetic data too.

LEFT / Leary decoded the magnetic strips on London Underground train tickets that hold information about the commuter's journey. The data she amassed provided insights into the user's everyday routine.

BELOW / Ferrofabric combines material science with traditional textile craft, showing the potential for surfaces and fabrics to be creatively reconfigured.

explore how textiles can cross over into areas such as material science, art and modern craft. 'Because magnetism is so central to modern technologies, I find that Ferrofabric easily enters into the art/science dialogue,' Leary says. For an art event, Leary set up an installation based on decoding the magnetic strips on London Underground train tickets that hold information about the commuter's journey. Leary could use the same kind of technology to magnetically encode information about her products in the textiles themselves, rather than attaching a conventional product tag.

Ferrofabric seems certain to emerge as a hybrid form that fuses the rigours of material science with the expressiveness of craft. As it does so, future surfaces are less likely to be permanently fixed, and more likely to be creatively reconfigured. 'I hope that in time I will be able to launch a completely new system of textiles that radically revolutionizes the way we interact with our magnetic environment.'

OPPOSITE / Leary's products are handcrafted, yet are derived from technological innovations that enable her to adapt magnetic polarities for use in textile applications. The designs shown on these pages were created for Italian womenswear label Claudia Ligari.

ABOVE / This image shows how the application of a magnetic field can cause Leary's fabrics to move. The relationship between magnetism and fabrics excites Leary, particularly as its full potential is yet to be explored.

RIGHT / Metal has been worn on the body for many centuries. Chain mail made for warriors and knights was popular during the medieval period, and Paco Rabanne famously designed chain mail dresses in the 1960s. Leary's work is bringing metal back to the catwalk today.

Leary is excited by the relationship between magnetism and textiles, believing its full potential has yet to be explored.

THIS PAGE / Leary's materials and products are handcrafted. The magnetic polarities they contain trigger them to interact with each other to create new surface textures as the wearer moves. Magnetic forces create changes in the textile's surface, which can reveal new patterns and motifs. The designs shown here were created for Claudia Ligari.

LEFT & BELOW / Leary's jewellery designs perform unexpectedly as the magnets they contain cause them to move and even reconfigure. The necklaces shown here are handmade and include components that can be rearranged to suit the style of the garments they are worn with.

BOTTOM LEFT / Most of Leary's designs are handmade in her Ferrofabric lab, where she experiments with a wide range of magnetic substances. Leary experiments with gels, powders and tiny pieces of metal, such as the ones shown here, to give her fabrics the optimal weight and drape.

ABOVE / Leary's system of magnetic wall tiles are soft squares of translucent material that adhere easily to most surfaces. The tiles form the basis for an interactive system that includes a variety of themed components, enabling users to create their own designs.

LEFT / A range of magnetic substances, such as gels and powders, can be deposited on the magnetic wall tiles to create a wide variety of patterns and textures.

BELOW LEFT & RIGHT / Magnetic components are being placed on the wall tiles, building a layered tableau. The components can be detached and infinitely rearranged to create new scenes. The finished result is an interactive wall mural that can be constantly changed.

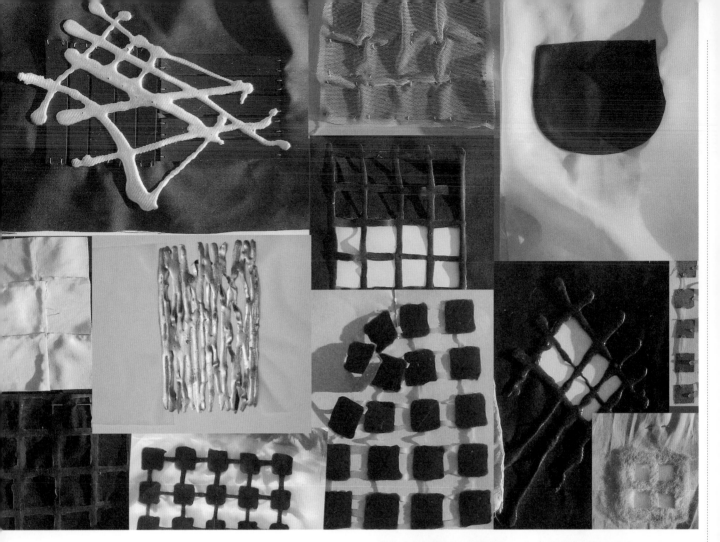

ABOVE / Leary experiments with different types of surface design to create novel textures and patterns. Each can contain a different magnetic polarity that affects its texture and performance.

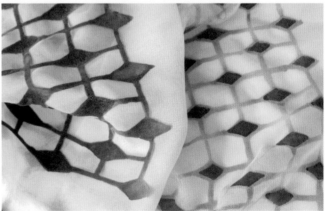

ABOVE / The Ferrofabric design here was created for Italian womenswear label Claudia Ligari.

THIS PAGE / The Encrypted Jewellery range includes pendants made from stones that contain 'invisible' designs. Leary created a technique that makes the designs appear on the surface before fading from view again.

RIGHT / Schicker's Glow textiles update traditional silk wallpaper. The Glow wallcoverings depict motifs inspired by flora and fauna, and light-emitting surfaces give them an ultra-contemporary twist.

OPPOSITE / Schicker's *Glow Bird* installation (a detail is shown here) was showcased at the Designer's Block pavilion at the Interiors 2010 trade show in Birmingham, UK.

KATHY SCHICKER

With their colour-changing surfaces, light-emitting fibres and interactive capabilities, the textiles created by London-based British designer Kathy Schicker are some of the most innovative fabrics made today. After training as a Jacquard weaver, Schicker now specializes in light-reactive textiles. Her work is driven by a fascination with light, materials research and the potential for merging traditional craft practices with cutting-edge technologies. As Schicker discovers the potential that photonics have for fabric applications, her work is also revealing new uses for photonic technology.

Recent advances in fibre technology have enabled textiles to gain ground in some of the industries where photonic technology is already established. Currently, photonic technology is widespread in diagnostic medical devices, data communication relays and laser-scanning technologies, where researchers are using textile techniques to make them wearable. Schicker is one of the first designers to recognize the creative potential that photonic technology holds for interior fabrics, artworks and decorative media. Schicker points out that, if developed for industrial applications, photonic textiles could be used

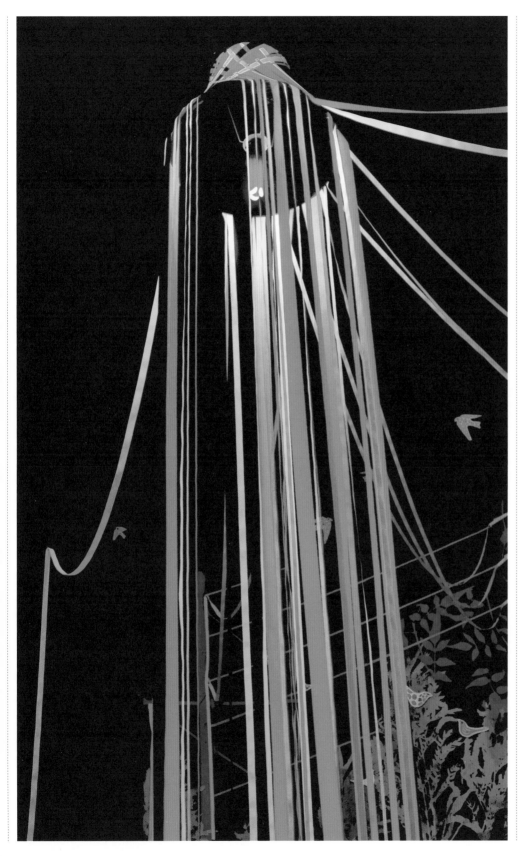

to craft signage or even enhance architectural facades.

So far, Schicker's research has resulted in new types of photonic fibres and a collection of colour-changing textiles. Her two main research projects to date are 'Woven Light', a series of colour-changing textiles, and a separate collection of photonic crystal fibre prototypes. The fabrics developed for the Woven Light series were created by integrating smart fibres into top-of-the-range woven Jacquard textiles. Each undergoes a reversible colour change when exposed to sunlight, or emits light in the dark. 'The fabrics have a magical quality,' Schicker says. 'The functional aspect is part of the material itself, meaning that only sunlight is needed to make the colour changes happen.' The colour changes vary according to levels of ambient light, evoking a wide spectrum of colours and tones. 'The fabrics are interactive, and constantly respond to the light conditions in the environment around them,' Schicker says. 'They are designed to be poetic and responsive by revealing different aspects of the design depending on the time of day.'

Working in collaboration with the physics department at the Polytechnique de Montréal, Canada, Schicker found ways to manipulate plastic photonic bandgap Bragg fibres developed by the department's researchers. 'These fibres have a number of unique functions,' Schicker says. 'Not only are they flexible; they do not require any surface abrasion to emit light. They can appear to be a particular colour when viewed under ambient light, yet project a different colour when light is channelled through the fibre itself. Because the relative light intensities of the fibres can be controlled, it may be possible to find applications for them in smart textiles, signage and works of art.'

Schicker's research reveals the impact that fibre research can have on other disciplines. Although the changes that occur in Schicker's fabrics are visually spectacular, they are created easily through the application of materials and light. Schicker explains 'Now that I understand what photonic technology can do, I can design a wide variety of textiles that utilize it. There are lots of applications for this work. It's great fun shedding light on the ones that work the best.'

THIS PAGE & OPPOSITE PAGE, BOTTOM / Schicker's *Bird* installation, is part of the Glow series. It is a large-scale wallcovering that uses fluorescent pigments to enhance the design details. The effect is that of a glow-in-the-dark installation that can decorate any interior where light levels are deliberately low.

OPPOSITE PAGE, TOP / Schicker crafted these lampshades from fabrics that sense fluctuations in light levels and change with them. The lampshades reveal different motifs depending on the time of day and the ambient light around them.

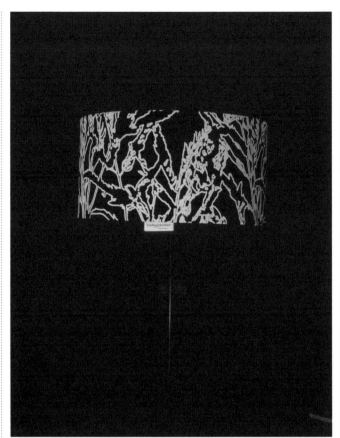

ABOVE LEFT & RIGHT / Working collaboratively with the physics researchers at the Polytechnique de Montréal, Canada, Schicker developed innovative ways of manipulating photonic crystal fibres to create a new generation of optic fibres. Most of the fibres appear to be colourless or white (shown right), but can easily be manipulated to transmit colour (shown left).

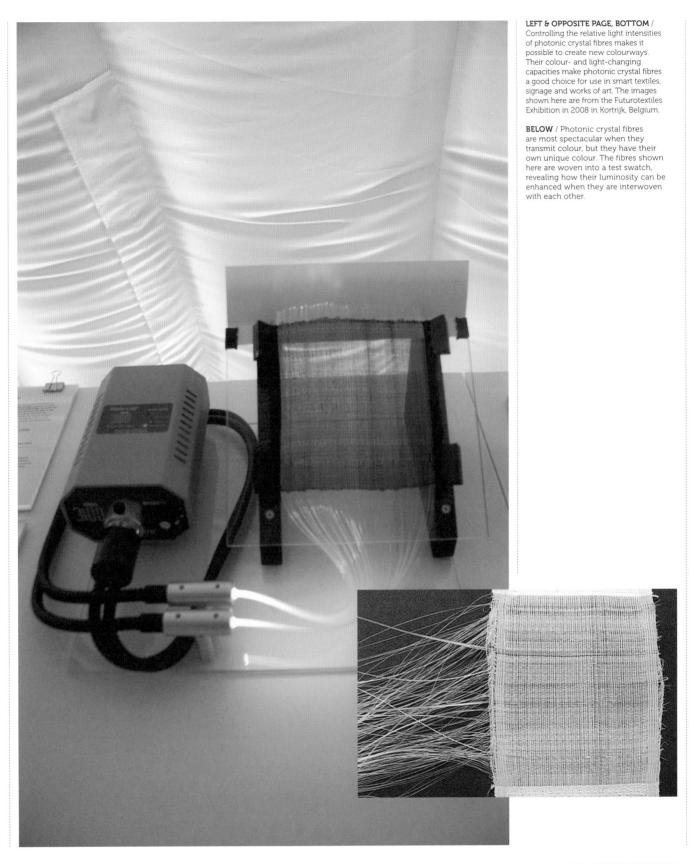

LEFT & OPPOSITE PAGE, BOTTOM /
Controlling the relative light intensities
of photonic crystal fibres makes it
possible to create new colourways.
Their colour- and light-changing
capacities make photonic crystal fibres
a good choice for use in smart textiles,
signage and works of art. The images
shown here are from the Futurotextiles
Exhibition in 2008 in Kortrijk, Belgium.

BELOW / Photonic crystal fibres
are most spectacular when they
transmit colour, but they have their
own unique colour. The fibres shown
here are woven into a test swatch,
revealing how their luminosity can be
enhanced when they are interwoven
with each other.

RIGHT / The light-reactive fabric shown here appears white until it is exposed to sunlight. UV rays enable it to change colour by day or glow in the dark. Schicker used the fabric to create a range of interior products.

BELOW / Schicker's Glow textiles are designed to be visible in both light and dark. The textiles are made in a range of colours and motifs that are eye-catching by both night and day.

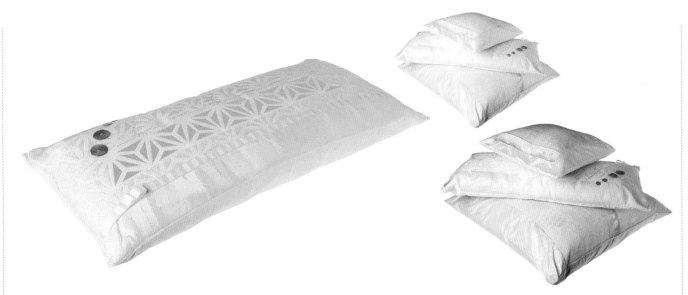

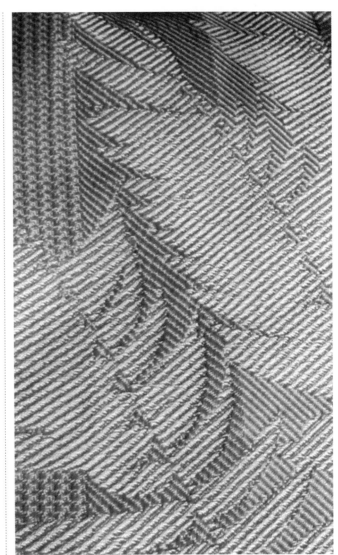

ABOVE / Schicker's light-reactive textiles are made into a range of interior accessories. These cushions and pillows have different appearances according to the light around them.

RIGHT / This detail reveals the beauty of the motif and the intricacy of the weave of the light-reactive fabric.

Kathy Schicker is driven by a fascination with light, materials research and the potential to merge traditional craft practices with cutting-edge technologies.

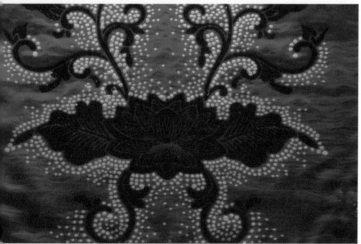

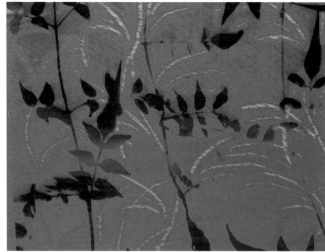

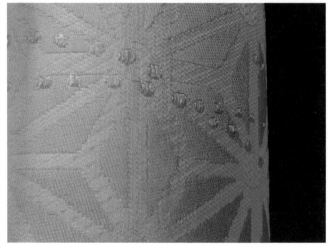

ALL IMAGES / The textiles shown here appear to be white until exposed to sunlight, which triggers their colours and patterns to emerge. Made into cushions, curtains, textile screens and upholstery fabrics, they transform an interior into an ever-changing, interactive space as they constantly respond to fluctuations in the light levels around them.

RIGHT / As she develops new ways of making garments more individual, Wallace is exploring the exchanges between the construction of cloth and printed textile design. New techniques that combine structure and surface in a single expression give fabrics a rich and unusual texture.

OPPOSITE / Wallace calls her method of creating richly textured textile surfaces 'patterning', which may one day revolutionize the manufacturing of clothing made from wool, denim, leather and nylon.

KERRI WALLACE

Fibre technology and high-performance designs are hallmarks of sportswear, a genre that has long been a market leader in textile innovation. British textile designer Kerri Wallace is taking sportswear design to a higher level today, as she develops high-tech textiles for performance applications. By combining smart textiles with printing technologies robust enough to be worn comfortably on an active body, Wallace creates responsive textiles that form wearable displays.

Wallace is currently a PhD student at Loughborough University, where she is exploring combined laser/dye methods for textile coloration and patterning techniques. She also has a separate ongoing research project developing responsive textiles that sense the wearer's movements and register changes on the fabric's surface. 'I call this research area "Motion Response Sportswear",' Wallace says. 'The physical energy expended during exercise creates body heat, which I harness using heat-sensitive technology I have integrated into screen printed textiles developed for sportswear. Digital print technology can be adapted to apply materials such as thermochromic inks, which respond to body heat.' To help

prevent them from becoming overheated or experiencing muscle fatigue the athletes will monitor the changes that occur on the textile surfaces. Wallace's system could help athletes prevent muscle burn or getting cramp, and could highlight parts of the fabric that rub against the skin or chafe the wearer.

The printing processes that Wallace is pioneering create new methods of integrating technology into sportswear textiles. Combined with smart media, the printing process facilitates sensory communication between body and fabric: overall body temperature and the heat emitted by 'hot spots', such as the solar plexus, can be detected via body heat and trigger changes on the fabric's surface. 'The Motion Response system utilizes thermochromic and liquid crystal heat-responsive technology' Wallace says. 'The sensory material is primarily heat-sensitive ink, which may be used both to decorate the garment and to provide information about the wearer without needing additional gadgetry to make it work. My work focuses on integrating low-tech technology in fabric and developing new printing methods to create smart, wearable garments. As a designer, I am merging creativity and technology to achieve a seamless integration of high- and low-tech approaches.'

A wide range of new materials and technologies common in fashion today were originally developed for use in the area of high-performance sportswear. Fashion designers are using sportswear fabrics to create multi-functional garments that look stylish enough to wear on the high street, yet are comfortable and elastic enough to wear while working out. This reveals the potential for the printing methods and sensory systems being engineered by Wallace to find applications in mainstream fashion once they have taken hold in sportswear.

Wallace is also developing new printing methods for her 'Garment ID' project, which seeks fresh applications for traditional and technological image-making methods. As she updates conventional image-making processes, Wallace is developing ways to give individual garments a unique identity. 'I'm exploring the interplay between cloth and printed textile design to establish a platform for the design and development of hybrid performance clothing,' Wallace says. 'Identity, use and value of a functional garment are being investigated as a result. I'm currently creating a capsule wardrobe that initiates the basis for new methods of making patterns in textile imaging and print design.'

As she integrates technology and high-performance textiles, Wallace's work is encouraging the movement of materials and technologies across disciplines. Motion Response Sportswear's sensory systems may also have potential uses for healthcare textiles, as they could be adapted to detect the wearer's vital signs. 'The textiles I'm designing can be used in many ways,' Wallace says. 'They can contribute to a healthier lifestyle, and if worn with awareness, can help the wearer find the right balance of work and play.'

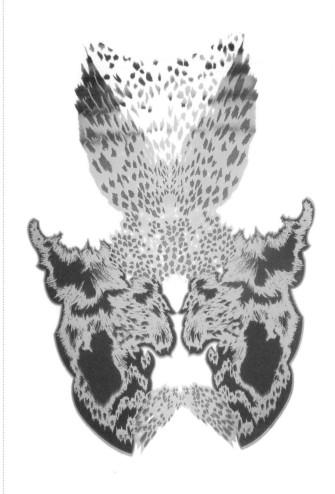

ABOVE LEFT & RIGHT / The combination of thermochromic inks and advanced textile technologies enables Wallace to create clothing that is dynamic and reactive. The motif shown here is transferred onto fabric using thermochromic inks to create a colour-changing effect.

Kerri Wallace combines thermochromic inks and advanced textile technologies to create high-performance clothing that interacts with the wearer.

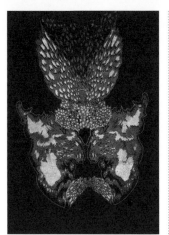

RIGHT / These three images capture how a pattern begins to emerge as body heat activates the thermochromic inks printed on the fabric.

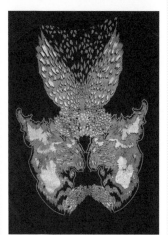

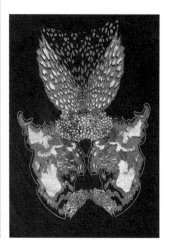

LEFT / As Wallace pioneers new ways of printing textiles made for performance sportswear, she is also exploring the extent to which wearable displays and colourful motifs (such as the one shown here) can be applied to fabric. Wallace has worked in consultation with the Inkjet Research Centre at the University of Cambridge and brands such as Speedo, Polartec and Triumph.

RIGHT / Wallace is using temperature-sensitive print technology via thermochromic materials to reconceive static patterns as wearable displays in textiles designed for sportswear. Wallace's research project is called Motion Response Sportswear and aims to revolutionize fitness apparel and mainstream fashion.

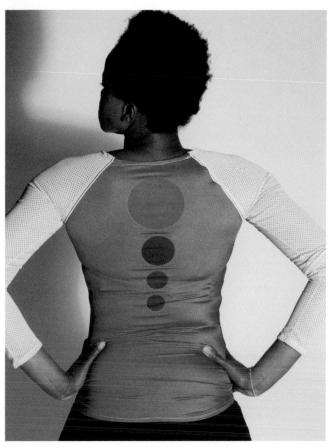

LEFT & BELOW / Round discs printed onto fabric with thermochromic inks change colour in response to the wearer's body temperature. Worn by an athlete, it becomes clear to trainers and team members when the wearer is overheating. Both garments shown here feature Wallace's multi-coloured thermochromic Bird Back motif, which morphs into three different colourways.

COLOUR DISSAPPEARS ABOVE:

green	25 0C	
orange	25 0C	
magenta	31 0C	
black	36 0C	
blue	50 0C	

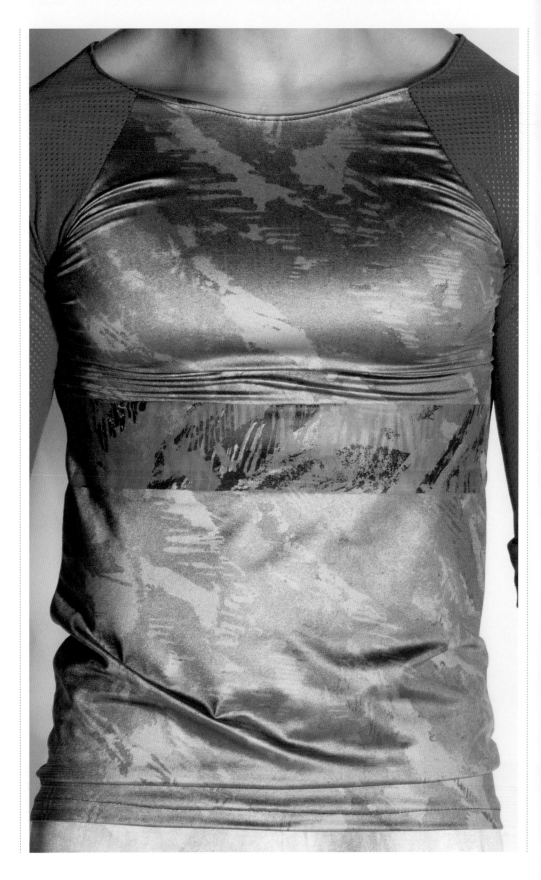

RIGHT / The development of sportswear textiles brings design, biology and technology together, and the new methods that result often introduce innovations to mainstream fashion. Although Wallace designed this motif for high-performance sportswear, its appeal as a fashion garment is obvious.

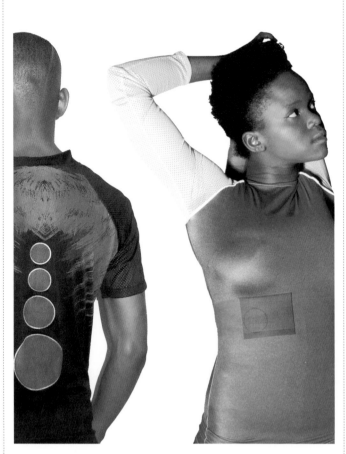

THIS PAGE / Wallace's thermochromic design methodology is in effect a diagnostic system that monitors correlations between heart rate and body temperature, then triggers a change on the fabric's surface. The motifs shown here demonstrate the wide range of Wallace's output, and reveal that wearable diagnostic displays can appear edgy and cool.

MARIA LÖW

Maria Löw is one of the best-known textile designers in Sweden today, and the interest in her work extends far beyond the country's borders. Löw was born in Stockholm, so it's no coincidence that her designs capture the capital's vibrancy and pulse, reflect the local art scene and draw inspiration from the waterways and forested parklands surrounding the city. Since making her debut on the design scene two decades ago, Löw's works have won awards in Sweden and elsewhere, been exhibited in galleries and museums and have achieved record-breaking sales worldwide.

Known for her ability to innovate, Löw has experimented with a variety of processes and techniques to create striking textiles for domestic interiors and commercial spaces. Löw has employed burn-out techniques to create lacy effects, creates textiles with varying thicknesses and pushes the rotation cycles in print machines to their limits in order to overprint edgy, unexpected motifs. Löw's works are often characterized by their painterly patterns or dramatic clashes of black and white. Strikingly graphic, but without overpowering the eye, Löw's designs are made to be minimal in style, but maximal in effect.

Swedish textile manufacturer Almedahls produces Löw's range of interior fabrics. One of the most visionary designs they have produced to date is Löw's hand-tufted '3D' carpet, fabricated with innovative cutting techniques that create trompe l'oeil effects. The carpet has a sense of perspective and depth, created by catching and reflecting light along its dense fibres. 'I wanted to create a carpet with light and shadow effects,' Löw explains. 'I had to innovate to make it work, as the yarn itself does not reflect light. By developing methods of cutting the wool against the fibre's grain, I found a way to create light and shadow contrasts throughout the surface of the carpet.'

The '3D' carpet was designed with public spaces and commercial areas in mind. 'Interior textiles provide a decorative function that everyone is used to,' Löw says. 'Our eyes are trained to look at them in a certain way. I wanted to take people by surprise, so I designed the carpet's surface in a way that would force the eye to look at it in a different way, which introduces a new way to experience a textile. Trompe l'oeil is more common in paintings, and sometimes seen in tapestries, but very rarely in hand-tufted surfaces.' When conventional hand-tufting techniques failed to produce the desired effect, Löw found a new way to fabricate the carpet. 'We built a maquette, which reproduced the carpet in wood,' Löw says. 'To get the angles of the cuts right on the surface, the workers had to lay the carpet on top of the maquette, which helped them find the right gradients to cut towards.'

Another one of Löw's hand-tufted designs is the 'Parquet' rug, which, like the '3D' carpet, is intended to trick the eye. 'Parquet is a conceptual design,' Löw explains. 'It's a soft surface that resembles a hard one, as if placing a rigid floor on top of

a pre-existing interior floor, or integrating the new one within the old. I created a pattern of lines that changes direction, and a colourway that includes only three tones. The effect it created was that of a flat surface, even though it is actually a richly textured, tufted one.' In order to create uniform fibre lengths that would make the carpet's surface appear even flatter, Löw commissioned a robot to tuft the carpet, loop by loop.

Löw's textured designs are born out of her ability to find new ways of looking at textile surfaces. By innovating with traditional processes, Löw makes time-honoured textile techniques work in surprising new ways. As Löw's designs continue to intrigue and inspire, they reveal the designer's ability to transform everyday surfaces into dynamic forms for contemporary life.

ABOVE / Cool, understated colours and pale textures characterize Löw's approach to interior designs. Löw uses colour and texture to catch light and reflect it, making small rooms (such as the one shown here) appear larger.

RIGHT / Simple, natural forms provide inspiration for many of Löw's motifs. Simple black-and-white contrast, such as the study for Löw's Kvitter textile, are strikingly graphic without being overpowering.

THIS PAGE / Löw designs window treatments alongside printed and woven fabrics, such as this Kvitter fabric, and makes hand-tufted carpets and specially commissioned textiles to order. Löw works with natural materials as well as technical fibres, resulting in fabrics imbued with utility as well as innovation, making them good choices for domestic interiors and commercial areas alike.

OPPOSITE PAGE / Löw's Acacia motif, shown here on a sheer curtain, captures the crisp outlines of leaves, which overlap to create painterly silhouettes.

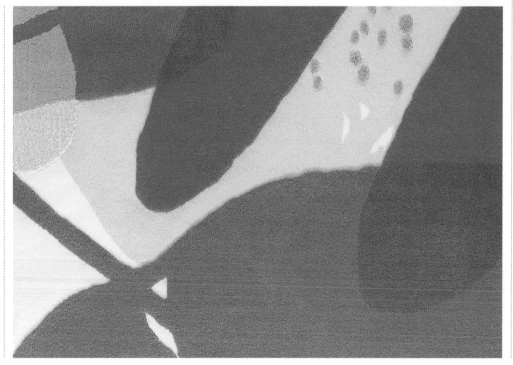

ABOVE LEFT / Löw's Blomstra motif, shown here on a sheer curtain, depicts an assemblage of spring flowers sketched in watercolours against a pale background.

ABOVE RIGHT & RIGHT / The motifs Löw creates are striking without overpowering the eye. Löw likes to overlay subtle shades of colour with bold outlines or transparent shapes, often combining two colours to create a third, or more, as shown in this tufted Acacia carpet.

OPPOSITE / Shown here in blue colourways, the Acacia tufted carpet has a strong graphic profile that is more characteristic of abstract art than traditional textile design.

Maria Löw uses burn-out techniques to create lacy effects, makes unexpected textures, and pushes the rotation cycles in print machines to their limits.

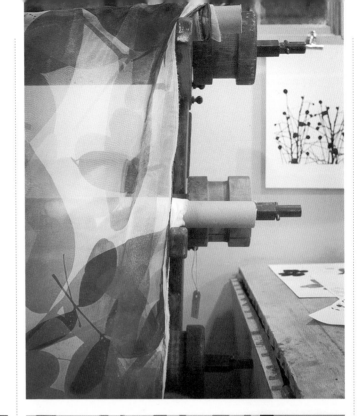

ALL IMAGES / Löw's work is often characterized by bold, uncompromising shapes sketched out within wide margins. Both natural forms and painted surfaces have inspired Löw since the start of her career, and she brings these together in her motifs. Löw's Haga design (opposite page), Acacia (right), Sonja (below) and Lace (below right) are minimal in style yet maximal in impact.

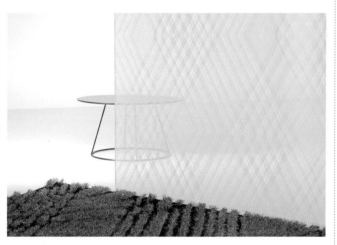

LEFT & ABOVE RIGHT /
Löw's signature Lace motif has
been produced in a range of fabrics,
textures and colourways. The motif
has been scaled up and super-sized to
create the carpet patterns (left), and
printed in pale colours to create the
curtain (above).

ABOVE / Löw's Corso motif, seen on
the curtain shown here, was inspired
by a trip to Scotland, where she was
fascinated by tartan. As a result, Löw
created this checked 'burn-out' curtain,
a design that takes the classic sheer
curtain in a contemporary direction.

LEFT / The overlapping leaves of lush clover inspired this eponymously named Love curtain. The motif is created from intersecting parallel lines.

BOTTOM LEFT / The Vico rug is handtufted in wool and flax and was inspired by the leafy olive groves and rolling hills of Calabria, where Löw lives and works during the summer months.

BOTTOM RIGHT / Löw's 3D carpet has a sense of perspective and depth, created by catching and reflecting light within its dense fibres. Löw experimented with wool-cutting techniques to develop the carpet, going against the wool's resistance to create light and shadow contrasts.

OPPOSITE / NunoErin's interactive felt fabric Raw, shown here, is an interior wall fabric that integrates handmade felt with LED lighting and touch sensors. The textile was made to revive the appeal of felt, and integrates technological components to boost its tactile and visual appeal.

RIGHT / This detail of Raw highlights the materials it is made from. Spelsau fibres, merino fleece and mohair locks are visible on the surface, chosen for their ability to absorb and reflect light.

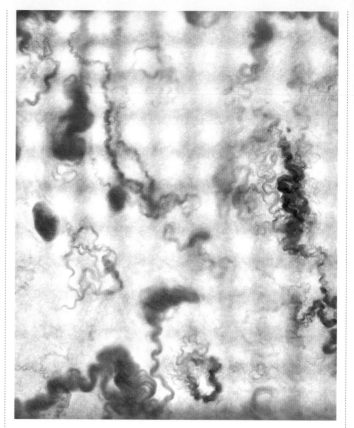

NUNOERIN

In 2006, when Erin Hayne and Nuno Gonçalves Ferreira established their design studio, the applications for colour-changing materials were virtually unexplored. Hayne and Gonçalves Ferreira say they set out to 'bring sensory experiences to everyday objects', which led them to materials and technologies that could change colour on contact. 'We were attracted to the chance interactions thermosensitive spaces create,' Hayne says. 'Thermosensitive materials allow people to use their body to mark a brief moment in time. It is an elegant way to register your presence and leave evidence of your interactions behind you.'

Hayne and Gonçalves Ferreira named their studio NunoErin, then moved into a restored warehouse in Jackson, Mississippi, where they could mix and match colours, dyes, materials and found objects. They began by injecting colour-changing inks into foam, which they moulded into interactive floor cushions. They also combined thermochromic inks with rubber, which they used to coat the moulded foam. The thermochromic surface that resulted created an imprint when touched, leaving a temporary mark. The imprint resembles a 'negative', such as those seen on film transparencies, which may appear to be entirely monochrome, or tinged with faint colours.

NunoErin embarked on collaborations with companies such as Sommers Plastics, a manufacturer of synthetic

textiles, who use colour-changing crystals. Sommers Plastics successfully incorporated the crystals into fabric, which enabled NunoErin to develop a textile suitable for use as an interior fabric. 'Our first application was upholstered seating,' says Gonçalves Ferreira, 'which we chose so that people could experience the material with their entire body.' Since then, NunoErin have extended their repertoire to include other materials, such felt made from spelsau, merino fleece, mohair and silk. 'Our felt fabric is interactive,' Hayne says. 'We built layers with the different materials in ways that would alternately absorb and reflect light. Sensors and LEDs were integrated into the felt to detect conductive objects, such as the human body, and make the fabric light up.'

Although the effects that NunoErin's materials create are striking, their designs are more than surface deep. NunoErin also use their materials and design expertise to solve real problems. 'Healthcare is one of our research areas,' Hayne says. 'Thermosensitive sports clothing can provide valuable feedback for athletes, showing them immediately if they risk overheating or, if worn in cold climates, contracting hypothermia.' Fieldwork with researchers in the medical sector has revealed the potential for thermochromic prescription labels and medicine bottles. 'That would be particularly relevant for medicine that must be kept within a cool temperature range to remain effective. Once they got too warm, the colour would permanently change, or disclose

a hidden warning message.'
One of the most unexpected
discoveries NunoErin made was
finding out that thermochromic
materials are therapeutic for
children with special needs. 'Our
thermosensitive stools are being
used by teachers and therapists
working with children that have
conditions such as autism,' Hayne
says. 'The process of touching
thermosensitive surfaces and
watching the handprints appear
has been used to demonstrate
cause and effect. It helps the
children differentiate between
colours and aids in tactile
stimulation and self-awareness.'
Although NunoErin's products
fulfil functional roles, Hayne and
Gonçalves Ferreira think their
appeal lies in their ability to
be played with. 'We think that
thermosensitive materials appeal
to the senses in lots of ways,
and can be enjoyed for their
playful properties,' Hayne says.
'They have proved to be truly
therapeutic, not just for children
with particular needs, but also
for adults wanting to switch off
and recharge their batteries. We
believe that regardless of the
audience, the strength of our
materials is in the connections
they can make between body
and mind.'

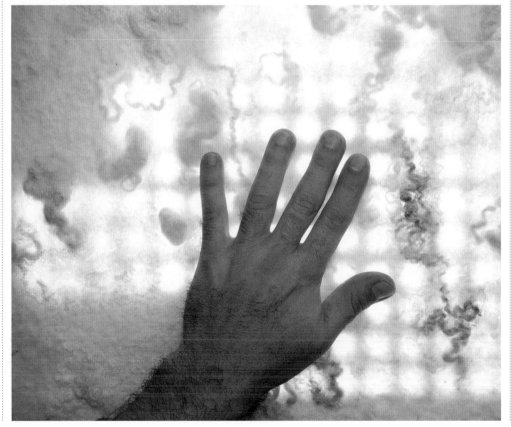

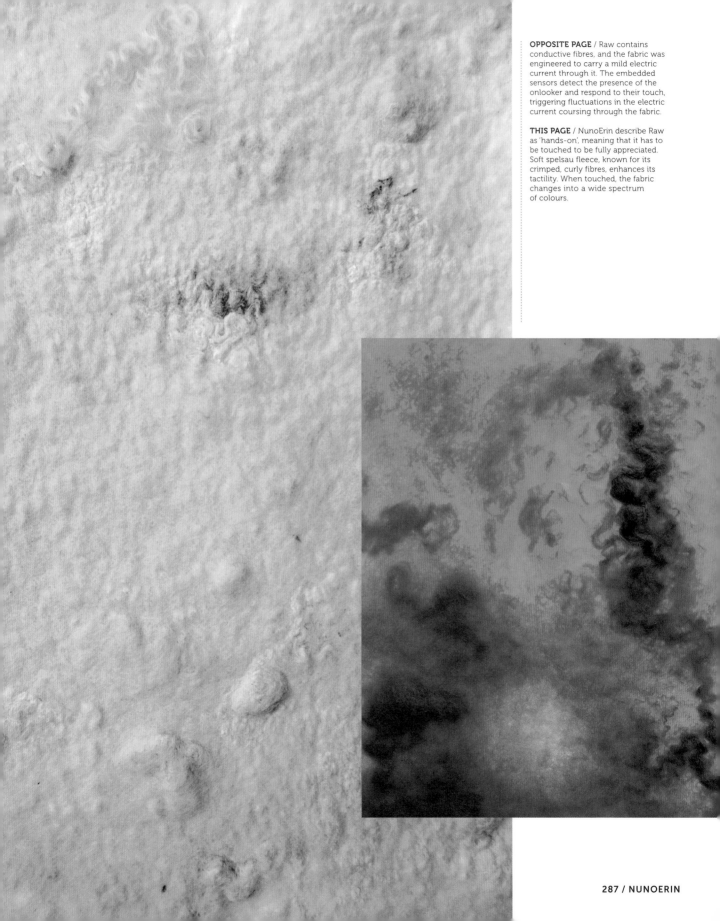

OPPOSITE PAGE / Raw contains conductive fibres, and the fabric was engineered to carry a mild electric current through it. The embedded sensors detect the presence of the onlooker and respond to their touch, triggering fluctuations in the electric current coursing through the fabric.

THIS PAGE / NunoErin describe Raw as 'hands-on', meaning that it has to be touched to be fully appreciated. Soft spelsau fleece, known for its crimped, curly fibres, enhances its tactility. When touched, the fabric changes into a wide spectrum of colours.

NunoErin integrate sensors and LEDs
into soft felted wool, enabling the fabric
to detect conductive objects, such as the
human body, which triggers the textile
to light up.

OPPOSITE / NunoErin's Touch wall panels are modular fabric components that change colour in response to body heat, creating an impression of the person interacting with them. The impressions remain vivid for several seconds before slowly fading, then disappearing entirely.

RIGHT / Heat-reactive fabric can reveal a wide spectrum of colours. The Touch wall panels shown here show blue shifting to purple and red transforming into violet, while orange is becoming yellow.

BELOW / NunoErin's organically shaped stool Swamp, shown here, is upholstered in the signature heat-reactive fabric. A single touch is enough to trigger a temporary change in the fabric, which can also change colour when ambient heat levels rise.

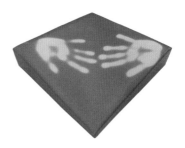

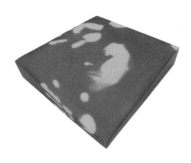

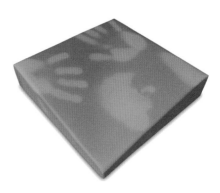

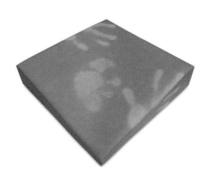

RIGHT / Veja weaves fabrics containing shape-malleable yarns that she programmes to morph into elaborate 3D shapes. Her Pop Pleat fabric alternates between a smoothly textured flat surface and a pleated shape.

OPPOSITE PAGE / Veja's fabrics are characterized by movement, which she creates through use of technological yarns and complex woven structures. The Bounce fabric shown here transforms into a new shape, then reverts to its original form.

PRITI VEJA

Textile design and engineering may seem like an incompatible mix, but together they are transforming the way fabrics can move and appear. Working as a researcher in the School of Engineering and Design at Brunel University, London-based designer Priti Veja is applying principles of mechanization to textile design, enabling fabrics to move and illuminate as a result. Veja uses shape-malleable yarns to weave fabrics that morph into elaborate three-dimensional structures when designed to do so. Electroluminescent lighting technology is integrated into the textiles to simultaneously heighten their aesthetic properties and tactile appeal. Endowed with characteristics seldom found in conventional fabrics, Veja's textiles look, feel and perform unlike any other fibre-based object.

Veja's interest in transformable textiles emerged during her undergraduate degree at Central Saint Martins and evolved further into an advanced collection during her MA studies at the Royal College of Art, when she integrated materials such as cellophane, polyester, wire, reflective yarn and polyurethane-coated yarn into fabrics to make them tensile. 'While at the Royal College, I began extending the boundaries of materials and structures in woven textiles,' Veja says. 'Innovating with new techniques and technological materials challenges the traditional view of flat, smooth two-dimensional textiles. I created my 'Transformables' collection during my MA studies, which were inspired by the idea of movement, particularly through mechanical transitions

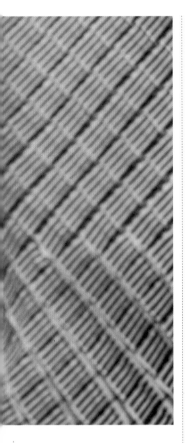

in objects. What sets my fabrics apart from many others in this genre is that I make the transitions fully reversible, enabling them to transform into a new shape, then revert to their starting points again.'

The transformable structures Veja creates are formed from conventional weaving techniques, which enable her to integrate technologized materials. 'Woven structures and threading drafts were actually designed to facilitate manipulations, which is how specific weaves, and hence, particular types of cloth are created,' Veja says. 'The weaves provide me with a pre-existing template that I can challenge and manipulate.' Veja's engineering know-how enables her to determine the placement of specific yarns and

woven structures in selected areas. As the layers of woven fibres begin to take shape, the textile's structure is formed, and completed with the addition of soft technological parts and advanced materials. 'My textiles require more pre-planning then conventional woven fabrics,' Veja explains. 'Figuring out complex geometries through modelling them in paper helps translate the ideas into visual structures. Prototyping is essential to a successful outcome.'

Although Veja's transformable textiles can change shape without requiring user involvement, they are designed to be interactive. 'The transition from one aesthetic to the next involves manually interacting with the piece,' Veja explains. 'Some of my early designs were exhibited in ways that engaged the spectators by inviting them to pull cords that sparked a transformation from one aesthetic state to another. The popularity of those textiles enabled me to discover what an important role individual interaction plays in the fabrics I create.'

One of Veja's working innovations is the development of a woven textile that enables visually impaired users to experience fabrics in new ways. 'I created a non-visual dimension by developing sensual tools that adults and children with visual challenges can relate to,' Veja says. 'The fabric gives heightened sensory feedback through its tactile and malleable qualities, which those with visual impairments can experience through their sense of touch. They can engage with the fabrics for a tactile experience, or adapt the textiles to facilitate many day-to-day activities where touch has to replace sight.'

Today, Veja is widening the scope of her research to find ways of integrating electronics into her textiles that connect to and interact with other systems. 'Integrating electronics into woven textiles creates soft technological interfaces,' Veja says. 'Synchronizing fabrics with other technologized objects adds another dimension altogether. My fabrics are often designed and constructed in multiple layers, and as I take them forwards, I'd like to make the applications and potential uses of them equally multifaceted.'

OPPOSITE / To enable her textiles to move, Veja uses advanced fibres and integrates technological yarns into them. Here, shape malleable yarns are interwoven to allow for structural manipulations of the textile.

LEFT / The Pop Pleat fabric is a complex, woven textile that changes shape as it triggers 3D structures to rise out of its flat surface. As it changes shape, it forms a different aesthetic and creates a new tactile experience.

BELOW / As the Pop Pleat fabric changes shape, new colours and motifs hidden within the fabric's folds are revealed, as this detail of the fabric shows.

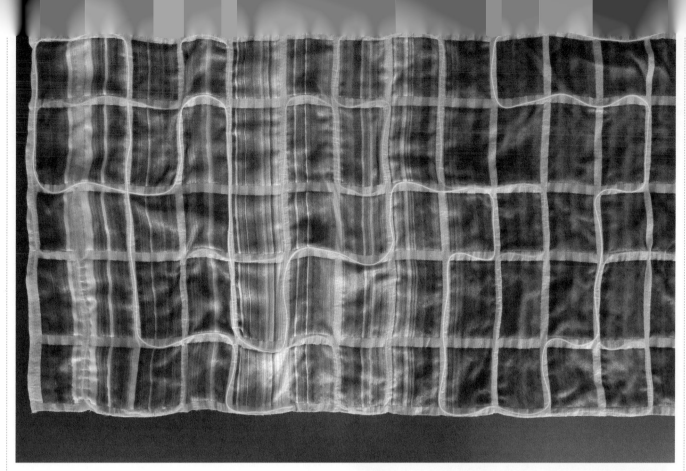

THIS PAGE / This woven textile is made with electroluminescent thread, making it eye-catching and unique. Electroluminescent thread is luminous, soft and colourful, as the detail on the right shows.

OPPOSITE, LEFT / This detail from Veja's Multi-Pleat shows the range of colours revealed when it opens its pleats.

OPPOSITE, RIGHT / Woven from soft fibres and conductive threads, the Pop Tube is a luminous woven shape that creates a soft light source.

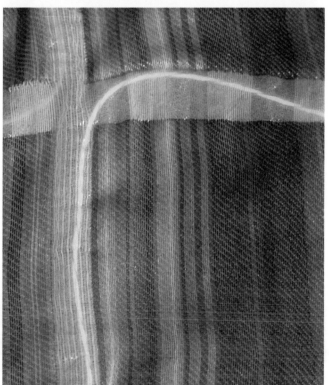

Priti Veja integrates shape-malleable yarns and electroluminescent lighting technology into textiles to heighten their aesthetic properties and boost their tactile appeal.

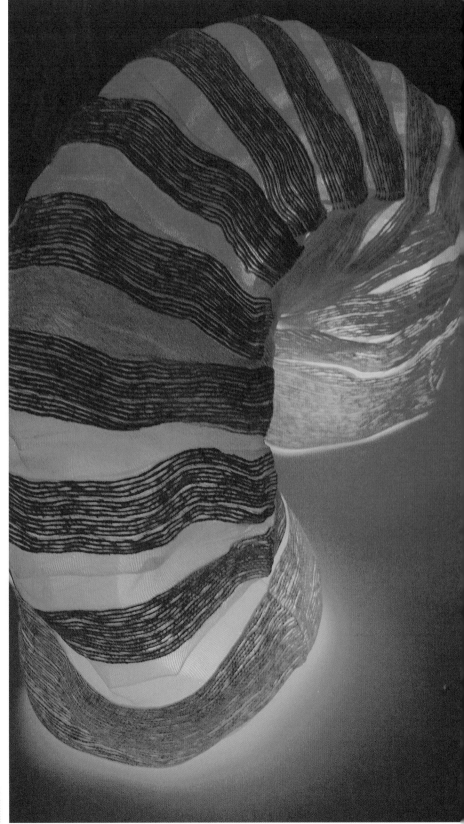

RIGHT / The White Sac is a woven form that contains reflective threads. This creates a luminosity of threads on the outer surface, as well as a unique glow inside formed by the metallic yarns.

BELOW / Veja's fabrics are engineered as much as they are designed and woven. Her Pop Pleat fabrics, shown here, move according to the placement of specific yarns and variations in the structure of the weave.

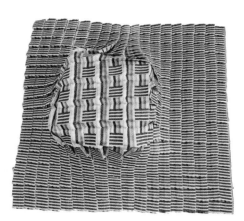

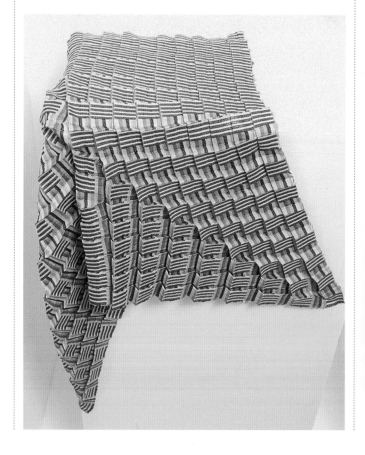

RIGHT / Veja's fabrics have the look, feel and performance of other textiles, but their mechanical abilities make them unique. The Kinetic Mono Module Pleats shown here can move autonomously.

BELOW / The Kinetic Pleat textile shown here opens slowly to reveal colours and textures woven into its structure.

BOTTOM RIGHT / Veja first sketches her fabrics, then prototypes them. This sketch depicts the Kinetic Mono Modules shown top right.

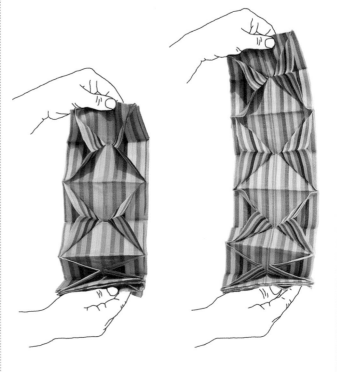

OPPOSITE, TOP / Skin Graph work
across multiple platforms. Textile
design, 3D digital design tools,
parametric modelling and fashion
pattern cutting techniques all come
together to create unique
laser-cut garments.

OPPOSITE, BOTTOM / Parametric
modelling software is used to map
out the topography of the body.
The software guides the modelling
tools along the body's contour lines,
creating a greyscale topography that
forms the basis for a digital pattern.

SKIN GRAPH

Good fashion fabrics create more than just a facade. They mould naturally to the wearer's physique and move with the body. Conventional body scanning technology and computer-aided design programmes can engineer a close fit, but forget to factor the wearer's posture and movements into the finished design. With that in mind, fashion designer Laura Michaels and architect Karl Kjelstrup-Johnson set up the creative platform called Skin Graph, which develops scanning technology and computational design techniques that map out the body on many levels.

Skin Graph use advanced computational strategies to scan the body. Imaging technology such as motion capture and 3D thermal scanning systems create avatar-like three-dimensional representations of the individual. The 3D representations are then relayed to a parametric modelling program, which maps out the body's contours much like a cartographer would chart a landscape and portray it on paper. The resulting template resembles a topographical diagram, representing the body mathematically and interpreting it as lines, cones, circles and spheres to form the basis of a dress pattern. The pattern that results is subsequently laser-cut into leather or cloth, which can then be stitched or bonded to create a unique garment. Skin Graph's clothing fits the wearer as well as any other tailor-made garment would, and has the advantage of moving with the body as though it is a second skin.

The parametric modelling program created by Skin Graph captures a wider range of data about the individual then conventional body scanners do. 'Our system maps the body on multiple levels, recording the gestures, postures and movements of the individual, and adjusts the design parameters accordingly,' Kjelstrup-Johnson explains. The garment is unique to wearer because it 'gives' in areas where the scan detects surface tension created by habitual postures or repeated movement. 'Conventional clothing is made to contain the wearer, but Skin Graph's designs are made to move with the body,' Kjelstrup-Johnson says.

As a fashion designer, Michaels is well versed in tailoring techniques as well as methods of manipulating fabric. 'Skin Graph's garments are structured by cuts in the fabric that enable the textile to move with the body,' Michaels says. 'The textile is cut and structured at the same time it is pattern cut, combining the process of manipulating the fabric with the one that cuts out the pattern. It's an innovative process that replaces conventional cutting techniques and market-led mandates.' Michaels believes that Skin Graph's model of parametric clothing provides a welcome respite from mainstream fashion. 'I like to challenge the trend-based fashions that are popular today,' she says. 'Skin Graph's garments are driven by individual styles and performance fits rather than echoing the styles that are popular for just one season. The season's choice of fabric and hence clothing choices are dictated by the industry, but Skin Graph gives the wearer more control over the style, look and fit they want.'

Just as Skin Graph's technology presents a platform for consumers to use, it also provides fashion brands with a new method of fabrication. 'Fashion brands with retail outlets could quickly create a bespoke garment by scanning their customers to make digital representations of them,' Kjelstrup-Johnson explains. 'Brands are recognizing the appeal that virtual versions of their garments have for web-based consumers. They could easily modify a virtual garment with the data gleaned from a parametric scan of an individual. The garment would then fit the wearer perfectly.'

Skin Graph can use their technology to create virtual garments, which can be tried on by the wearer's avatar in a virtual wardrobe. Because Skin Graph's technology is able to provide real-time feedback to the individual, it could compare pre-existing virtual garments to the wearer's body, and help them decide which ones should be purchased. 'Our work fuses the physical and the digital,' Kjelstrup-Johnson says. 'Not only will the process create a garment that can be manufactured in the real world, it also provides an intelligent design tool that has been tailored specifically for the user, by the user. It is paving the way for new fabrication methods, and empowers the consumer to play a bigger part in selecting the fabric and fashions they wear.'

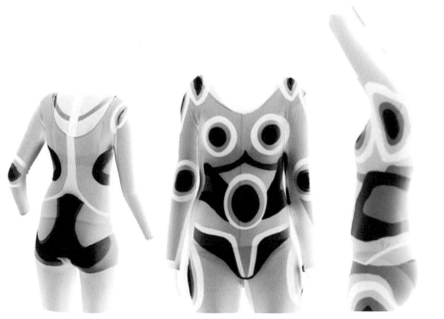

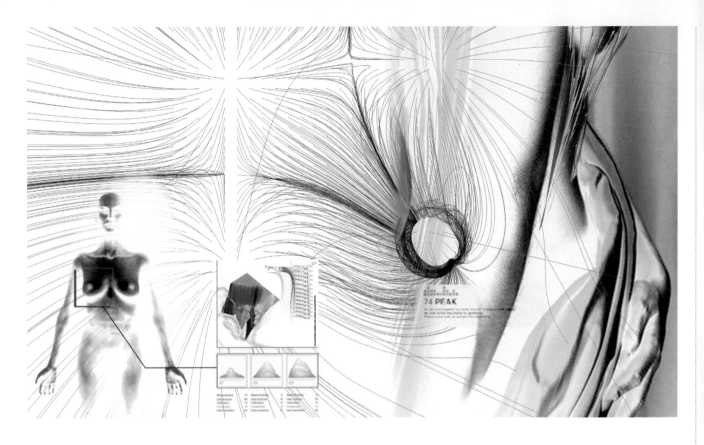

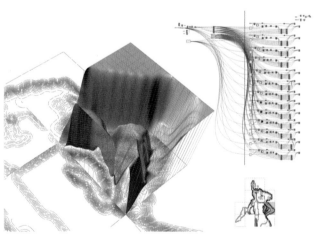

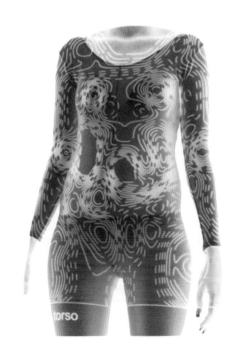

THIS PAGE / Laura Michaels combines her background in fashion design with parametric modelling tools to create a unique pattern for each client she scans. The lines and curves that result from the scan create a pattern and relay it to the laser-cutting tools.

Skin Graph's technology maps out the body on multiple levels, recording the gestures, postures and movements of the individual, and adjusts the design parameters accordingly.

ABOVE / the scanning process becomes a time for play and experimentation, allowing the individual a level of authorship over their bespoke clothing.

RIGHT / The scanning technology and computational design techniques that Skin Graph use map out the body on many levels. Here, a male subject was rendered from several perspectives to develop programs for the modelling software.

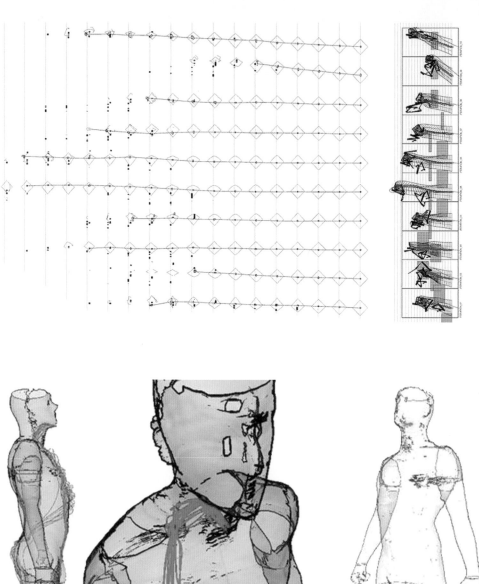

persp

ABOVE / The pattern created in Skin Graph's parametric modelling software was laser-cut into cloth, then stitched and bonded to create this one-off dress. Skin Graph's clothing designs are sized to fit the wearer just as other tailor-made garments are, but move with the body as though they were second skins.

RIGHT / Not all of Skin Graph's garments are form-fitting. The parametric modelling tools can be adjusted to incorporate draping, pleating or 'loose fit' options into the design. Skin Graph strive to map out more than just the wearer's physique; they try to capture the wearer's posture, movements and personality and incorporate it into the design. Clients are invited to slouch, cross their arms, shift their weight and even strike a sexy pose when being scanned.

Loose Fit

Draped

Comfort

Teasing

Silk Touch

Seductive

Body Landscape

Articulated Activation

Tailored Fit

TEXTILE DESIGNER DIRECTORY

KELSEY ASHE

www.ashestore.com.au
info@ashestore.com.au

JOANNA BERZOWSKA

www.xslabs.net
info@xslabs.net

LEAH BUECHLEY

High-Low Tech Group, MIT Media Lab
77 Massachusetts Avenue, E14/E15
Cambridge MA 02139-4307
USA
tel +1 617 253 2870
hlt.media.mit.edu
leah@media.mit.edu

CAROLE COLLET

Central Saint Martins
Granary Building, 1 Granary Square
King's Cross
London N1C 4AA
tel +44 20 7514 7444
www.carolecollet.com
c.collet@csm.arts.ac.uk

EMILY CRANE

www.emilycrane.co.uk
info@emilycrane.co.uk

CUTECIRCUIT

144 Shoreditch High Street
London E1 6JE
United Kingdom
tel +44 20 7502 1994
www.cutecircuit.com
cute@cutecircuit.com

GIADA DAMMACCO

Grado Zero Espace
Via Nove 2/A -50056 Montelupo F.no
Florence, Italy
tel +39 0571 80368
www.gzespace.com
giada.dammacco@gzespace.com

DAVA NEWMAN

Department of Aeronautics and Astronautics
33-307, Massachusetts Institute of Technology
77 Massachusetts Avenue
Cambridge, MA 02139
USA
tel +1 617 258 8799
dnewman@mit.edu

SHEREE DORNAN

Love in Tokyo
61-63 High Street
Fremantle 6160
Western Australia
tel +61 8 9433 2110
www.loveintokyo.com.au
info@loveintokyo.com.au

INDIA FLINT

PO Box 209
Mount Pleasant 5235
South Australia
www.indiaflint.com
appaloosa9@me.com

EUNJEONG JEON

eunjeong.jeon@postgrad.curtin.eud.au

VERONIKA KAPSALI

www.mmttextiles.com
info@mmttextiles.com

VALÉRIE LAMONTAGNE

www.3lectromode.com
valerie@3lectromode.com

BARBARA LAYNE

Studio SubTela
Hexagram Concordia
1515 St Catherine St West
EV 11-455.
Montreal, Quebec, H3G 2W1
tel +1 514 848 2424 ext 5939
www. subtela.hexagram.ca

JENNY LEARY

844 Laveta Terrace
Los Angeles
California 90026
USA
www.ferrofabric.com
jenny@ferrofabric.com

MARIA LÖW

Löw Design Sweden
Kvarngatan 3b
S-11847 Stockholm
Sweden
tel +46 86 4290 77
www.marialow.com
maria.low@marialow.com

PTOLEMY MANN

Studio 52, Clink Street Studios
1 Clink Street, Soho Wharf
London SE1 9DG
United Kingdom
tel +44 20 7357 7101
www.ptolemymann.com
fifth@ptolemymann.com

LAURA MARSDEN

3 Devon Mead
Hatfield, Herts
AL10 9GD
United Kingdom
www.lauramarsden.com

LUCY MCRAE

Lucy McRae Studio
Oudezijds Achterburgwal 79M
Amsterdam 1012 DC
The Netherlands
www.lucymcrae.net
info@lucymcrae.net

AURÉLIE MOSSÉ

www.aureliemosse.com
info@aureliemosse.com

NUNOERIN

533 Commerce Street
Jackson, MS 39201
USA
tel +1 601 944 0023
www.nunoerin.com
info@nunoerin.com

MAGGIE ORTH

1439 East Ward Street
Seattle, WA 98112
USA
tel +1 206 860 5166
www.maggieorth.com
morth@ifmachines.com

DESPINA PAPADOPOULOS

Studio 5050
PMB 386–315 Bleecker Street
NYC 10014
USA
tel +1 914 613 3491
www.5050ltd.com
emailme@5050ltd.com

HAYES RAFFLE

www.hayesraffle.com
info@hayesraffle.com

ISMINI SAMANIDOU

www.isminisamanidou.com
ismini@isminisamanidou.com

KATHY SCHICKER

tel +44 (0) 7904 197595
www.kathyschicker.com
kathyschicker@gmail.com

MARGO SELBY

4–11 Galen Place, Pied Bull Yard
London WC1A 2JR
United Kingdom
tel +44 207 242 6322
www.margoselby.com
info@margoselby.com

SABINE SEYMOUR

www.moondial.com

SKIN GRAPH

tel +44 750 6688920
www.skingraph.wordpress.com
karl@skingraph.co.uk

HELEN STOREY

www.helenstoreyfoundation.org
info@helenstoreyfoundation.org

STRETCHABLE CIRCUITS

Frohnauer Strasse 40a
13467 Berlin
Germany
tel +49 30 7071 8365
www.stretchable-circuits.com
info@stretchable-circuits.com

REIKO SUDO

www.nuno.com
info@nuno.com

NANCY TILBURY

tel +44 208 6160 872
studionancytilbury.com
info@studionancytilbury.com

PRITI VEJA

pritiveja@hotmail.com
www.weft-lab.com

KERRI WALLACE

www.kerriwallace.com
k.wallace@lboro.ac.uk

ADAM WHITON & YOLITA NUGENT

No-Contact LLC
1 Apple Hill, Suite 316
Natick, MA 01760
USA
www.no-contact.com
info@no-contact.com

INDEX

CREDITS

The author and publisher would like to thank the following for providing work and images for use in this book. In all cases every effort has been made to credit the copyright holders, but should there be any omissions or errors the publisher would be pleased to insert the appropriate acknowledgement in any subsequent editions of this book.

Front cover motif: Birds of Paradise; chapter opener motifs: Circus, Cherry Blossom and Alchemy prints. All by Kelsey Ashe.

Kelsey Ashe: all images courtesy of Kelsey Ashe. Ashe Papillion Dress, Tahiti Church print, Collections Perth Fashion Festival; Cherry Blossom Tunic, Collections Perth Fashion Festival; Cherry Blossom Gown, Phoenix Embroidery, Dragonflies, Ashe Casblanca Dress, Ashe Peony Silk Gown, Paradise Lost Print, Peonies Print, Swarm Print, Ashe Waratah Silk Tunic, White Waratah Print, Cockatoos Wallpaper Print, Fish Pollution Print, Fish Pollution Notebook. Photographers: Stefan Gossati, Yakub Erogul.

Joanna Berzowska, Skorpions: SKORPIONS, and XS Labs project by Joanna Berzowska and Di Mainstone with Marguerite Bromley, Marcelo Coelho, David Gauthier, Francis Raymond, and Valerie Boxer, photos by Nico Stinghe © XS Labs 2007; Captain Electric: Captain Electric and Battery Boy, an XS Labs project by Joanna Berzowska with Marc Beaulieu, Catou Cournoyer, Anne-Marie Laflamme, Vincent Leclerc, Catherine Marchand, Gaia Orain, and Emily Paris, photography by Guillaume Pelletier © XS Labs 2009; Karma Chameleon, SPARKL, and XS Labs project by Joanna Berzowska and Maksim Skorobogatiy with Marguerite Bromley and Marc Beaulieu, photography by Ronald Borshan, Joanna Berzowska and Marc Beaulieu © XS Labs 2010; Modular Pleated Lights, an XS Labs project by Joanna Berzowska and Maksim Skorobogatiy with Anne-Marie Laflamme, Marguerite Bromley, and Marc Beaulieu, photography by Karin Demeyer © XS Labs 2010.

Leah Buechley: photography by Leah Buechley; ModKit screenshot by Ed Baafi.

Carole Collet: p113 (above and right) Biolace research project at Central Saint Martins College of Art & Design © Carole Collet; p114-115 Suicidal Pouf showcased as part of the Medical Research Council 'Nobel Textiles' exhibition at the Institute of Contemporary Art in London, 2008 © Carole Collet, images courtesy of Simon Denton; p116: Pop Up Lace manufactured as a limited edition by Sakae for Warp Factor 2009, a CSM touring exhibition held in Tokyo, Guangzhou and London © Carole Collet; photo of lace loom courtesy of Sakae.

Emily Crane: images courtesy of Emily Crane Cultivated Couture.

Francesca Rosella, CuteCircuit Ltd: p22 & 23 © CuteCircuit, photography by Alena Jaskanka; p24 © CuteCircuit, photography by Alena Jaskanka;

p25, K-Dress © CuteCircuit, photography by Francesca Rosella; p26, 27 and 29, Safura, photography by Giel Domen (EBU); p28, Twirkle T-Shirts © CuteCircuit, photography by Ryan Genz.

Giada Dammacco, Grado Zero Espace Srl: p233 photography by MC Laren; p234 © Grada Zero Espace; p235 (top) photograph © NASA, (bottom) © Grada Zero Espace; p236-237 © Grada Zero Espace.

Sheree Dornan, Love in Tokyo: p188-193 and 195-197, photography by Sheree Dornan; p194 (far left) photography by Bonnie Doran; p194 (main picture) photography by Songy Knox.

India Flint: p133 (left and bottom) photographer and model Helen Lyôn; p134 and 135 (bottom), photography by India Flint, model Violetta Flint; p135 (top) photography by Hiroyasu Daido; all other images courtesy of India Flint.

Eunjeong Jeon: p222 (right), p224, p225 (inset), p227, p229, photography by Kyunghoon Kim; p233, p225 (main picture), p226, p228, p230, p231 photography by Eunjeong Jeon. Model throughout, Eunjoo Jeon.

Veronika Kapsali, MMT Textiles: images courtesy of MMT Textiles with Fay Marney and Julie Stephenson.

Valérie Lamontagne, 3lectromode; Asymmetrical Modern, photography by Sandra Lynn Bélanger; Flower Shopping Bag, photograph courtesy of the artist.

Barbara Layne, Studio subTela; p12 The Tornado Dress, photography by H. Khoshneviss; p13 Jacket Antics, all photographs by H. Khoshneviss; p14 Currente Calamo, (top) H. Khoshneviss, (bottom) C. Carman; p15 Currente Calamo, (top and bottom right) H. Khoshneviss, (bottom left) C. Carman; p16 Jacket Antics, all photographs H. Khoshneviss; p17 Jacket Antics, (top left) Mikey Siegel, (bottom left) Guy Hoffman, (right) H. Khoshneviss; p18 all photographs H. Khoshneviss (upper left is Jacket Antics; lower left and right column photographs are Blue Code); p20 Lucere, all photographs H. Khoshneviss; p21 The Tornado Dress, photograph by Mikey Siegel; p19 Wearable Absence, created by Barbara Layne and Janis Jefferies, photographs by H. Khoshneviss.

Jenny Leary, Ferrofabric; p246 & 247: images by Jenny Leary; p248 image by Jonathon Griggs for Claudia Ligari; p249 top image by Jenny Leary, lower image by Jonathon Griggs for Claudia Ligari; p250 all images for Claudia Ligari; p251 all images by Jenny Leary; p252 small image by Jenny Leary, centre image by Brian Dawson for Jenny Leary; p253 lower images by Joseph Rasch for Jenny Leary; p254-255 all images by Jenny Leary.

Maria Löw: p275 and 276 photography by Helen Pé, architect Jenny Frigren; p277-281 photography by Patric Johansson; p283 (bottom left) photography by Anna Skoog.

Ptolemy Mann, Woven Textile Art Limited: p172 Chromascope1, photography by Ptolemy Mann; p173 Monoliths picture by Toril Brancher; p174 Indigo Adras, photography by Ptolemy Mann; p175 Chroma Cushion and Armoire images courtesy of John Lewis PLC; p176 Process pictures by Jeremy Jeffs; p177 Ikat Collection images by Nicole Rowntree; p178-179 Circle picture by Ptolemy Mann; fashion photography by Alun Callender; wall-mounted artworks, Matt Monroe.

Laura Marsden: all images courtesy of Laura Marsden

Lucy McRae: all images courtesy of Lucy McRae, with thanks to Bart Hess.

Aurélie Mossé: p214 Reef, design by Aurélie Mossé, collaborators: Guggi Kofod, David Gauthier, photography by Mathilde Fuzeau; p216 top and right, Reef (work in progress), design and photography by Aurélie Mossé; p217 left, Reef, design Aurélie Mossé, collaborators: Guggi Kofod, David Gauthier, photography by Mathilde Fuzeau; below, Reef (simulation), design by Aurélie Mossé/Anders Deleuran, photography by Anders Deleuran; p218, Reef (work in progress), design and photography by Aurélie Mossé; p219 top right, Caresser dans le bon sens du poil, design: A.Blonder, Y.Gilad, A.Mossé, O.Barr and B.Bauer during Architectural Knitting Workshop by A. Karmon, M. R. Thomsen, Shenkar University, Tel Aviv, photography by Aurélie Mossé; right Ice-Fern, design by Aurélie Mossé, Mette Ramsgaard Thomsen, Karin Bech, photography by Mette Ramsgaard Thomsen; [Extra]ordinary Furniture, design by Aurélie Mossé, photography by Mathilde Fuzeau.

Dava Newman: BioSuit™devised and created by Dava Newman in association with MIT and NASA, design by Guillermo Trotti, A.I.A. Trotti and Associates Inc., fabrication by Dainese, Italy; sketches and renderings by Cam Brensinger. All images courtesy of Dava Newman.

Erin Hayne and Nuno Ferreira, NunoErin: all images courtesy of NunoErin.

Maggie Orth: 100 Electronic Art Years, Detail, photography by David Klugston © Maggie Orth; BarcodeMan, photography by David Klugston © Maggie Orth; Blip, photography by David Klugston © Maggie Orth.

Despina Papadopoulos: all images courtesy of Despina Papadopoulos.

Hayes Raffle: p238 © 2000 Daniel Rozin; p239 © 2004 James Tichenor; p240 (top) © 2003 Hayes Raffle, (bottom) 'Square Windframe' image © 1980 Tim Prentice; p241 © 2002 Mitchell Joachim; p242 (top left) Hayes Raffle, © 2002 MIT Media Lab, all other images on this page and p243 © 2004 Hayes Raffle; p244 (top) © 2003 Hayes Raffle, (bottom left) © 2004 James Tichenor, (bottom right) © 2002 Mitchell Joachim; p245 all images © 2002 Mitchell Joachim.

Ismini Samanidou: p142-147, photography by Ismini Samanidou; p148 and 149 photography by Toril Brancher.

Kathy Schicker: all images courtesy of Kathy Schicker.

Margo Selby: all images courtesy of Margo Selby.

Sabine Seymour, Moondial; p84-89 © Moondial; p90-91 © Lukas Gangsterer; p83 © Mark Glassner.

Karl Kjelstrup-Johnson, Skin Graph: all images courtesy of Skin Graph, www.skingraph.co.uk.

Helen Storey: p126 Early Experiments, Trish Belford; p127 red shot, Megastar Dress detail, Wonderland, courtesy Alex Maguire; Blue: Textile detail, Wonderland, courtesy Alex Maguire; p128 Field of Jeans at Newcastle University, photo Gavin Duthie; p128 small image, Field of Jeans at Chelsea College of Art & Design courtesy Jon Daughtry/dedass.com; p129 Oxidising Herself, courtesy Trish Belford, p130 Finished textile pieces for Herself (detail), Trish Belford; Herself on mannequin, Newcastle, Nik Daughtry/dedass.com.

Stretchable Circuits: p10 and p92 design by Novanex, photography by Sonago; p93 design by Raphael Schall, photography by Jonas Lindström; p94 design by Wolfgang Langeder, photography by Elisabeth Grebe; p95 Theresa Lusser, photography by Christian Rose; p96 design by Mareike Michel, photography by Christian Rose; p97 designer/photographer Stephanie Hornig; p98-99 designer MOON Berlin, photography by Patrick Jendrusch; p100+101 designer Synne Geiersdatter Frydenberg, photography by Andreas Velten.

Reiko Sudo, Nuno Corporation: photography by Sue McNab.

Nancy Tilbury, Studio XO: images courtesy of Nancy Tilbury; Digital Skins photography by Perry Curties; Fashion Phreaking photography by Ezzidin Alwan; Digital Draping photography by Ellie Laycock.

Priti Veja: Transformables; p290, 291 and 295-297 photography by Priti Veja; p294 photography by Toril Brancher.

Kerri Wallace: all images courtesy of Kerri Wallace.

Adam Whiton: all images courtesy of Adam Whiton and Yolita Nugent.

AUTHOR'S ACKNOWLEDGEMENTS

This book would not have been possible without the support of the designers featured in it. I thank each one of them for giving generously of their time to discuss their works, inspirations and future directions. I would also like to thank the book's editors for their commitment to the project, and for being so great to work with.

Textile Visionaries is dedicated to Carla Feldshuh, a friend of long standing who has always inspired me with her visionary approaches to art, fashion and life in general.